Great Casseroles

Robert Carrier

Hamlyn London · New York · Sydney · Toronto

Photographs in this series taken by Christian Délu, John Miller, Jack Nisberg, Iain Reid, Pipe-Rich
Design by Martin Atcherley for The Nassington Press Ltd.
Line drawings by Terri Lawler

Some material in this book has already been published in
The Robert Carrier Cookbook
Published in 1965 by
Thomas Nelson and Sons Ltd.
© Copyright Robert Carrier 1965

Published by
The Hamlyn Publishing Group Limited
London · New York · Sydney · Toronto
Astronaut House, Feltham, Middlesex, England

© Copyright Robert Carrier 1978

ISBN 0 600 32011 1

Printed in Italy

Contents

Notes on metrication

When making any of the recipes in this book, only follow one set of measures as they are not interchangeable.

In this book quantities are given in metric and Imperial measures. Exact conversion from Imperial to metric measures does not usually give very convenient working quantities and so the metric measures have been rounded off into units of 25 grams. The table below shows the recommended equivalents.

Ounces	Approx gram to nearest whole figure	Recommended conversion to nearest unit of 25
1	28	25
2	57	50
3	85	75
4	113	100
5	142	150
6	170	175
7	198	200
8	227	225
9	255	250
10	283	275
11	312	300
12	340	350
13	368	375
14	396	400
15	425	425
16 (1 lb)	454	450
17	482	475
18	510	500
19	539	550
20 (1¼ lb)	567	575

Note: When converting quantities over 20 oz first add the appropriate figures in the centre column, then adjust to the nearest unit of 25. As a general guide, 1 kg (1000 g) equals 2.2 lb or about 2 lb 3 oz. This method of conversion gives good results in nearly all cases, although in certain pastry and cake recipes a more accurate conversion is necessary to produce a balanced recipe.

Liquid measures

The millilitre has been used in this book and the following table gives a few examples.

Imperial	Approx ml to nearest whole figure	Recommended ml
¼ pint	142	150 ml
½ pint	283	300 ml
¾ pint	425	450 ml
1 pint	567	600 ml
1½ pints	851	900 ml
1¾ pints	992	1000 ml (1 litre)

Can sizes

At present, cans are marked with the exact (usually to the nearest whole number) metric equivalent of the Imperial weight of the contents, so we have followed this practice when giving can sizes.

Oven temperatures

The table below gives recommended equivalents.

	°C	°F	Gas Mark
Very cool	110	225	$\frac{1}{4}$
	120	250	$\frac{1}{2}$
Cool	140	275	1
	150	300	2
Moderate	160	325	3
	180	350	4
Moderately hot	190	375	5
	200	400	6
Hot	220	425	7
	230	450	8
Very hot	240	475	9

Notes for American and Australian users

In America the 8-oz measuring cup is used. In Australia metric measures are now used in conjunction with the standard 250-ml measuring cup. The Imperial pint, used in Britain and Australia, is 20 fl oz, while the American pint is 16 fl oz. It is important to remember that the Australian tablespoon differs from both the British and American tablespoons; the table below gives a comparison. The British standard tablespoon, which has been used throughout this book, holds 17.7 ml, the American 14.2 ml, and the Australian 20 ml. A teaspoon holds approximately 5 ml in all three countries.

British	American	Australian
1 teaspoon	1 teaspoon	1 teaspoon
1 tablespoon	1 tablespoon	1 tablespoon
2 tablespoons	3 tablespoons	2 tablespoons
$3\frac{1}{2}$ tablespoons	4 tablespoons	3 tablespoons
4 tablespoons	5 tablespoons	$3\frac{1}{2}$ tablespoons

An Imperial/American guide to solid and liquid measures

Solid measures

Imperial	American
1 lb butter or margarine	2 cups
1 lb flour	4 cups
1 lb granulated or castor sugar	2 cups
1 lb icing sugar	3 cups
8 oz rice	1 cup

Liquid measures

Imperial	American
$\frac{1}{4}$ pint liquid	$\frac{2}{3}$ cup liquid
$\frac{1}{2}$ pint	$1\frac{1}{4}$ cups
$\frac{3}{4}$ pint	2 cups
1 pint	$2\frac{1}{2}$ cups
$1\frac{1}{2}$ pints	$3\frac{3}{4}$ cups
2 pints	5 cups ($2\frac{1}{2}$ pints)

Introduction

French cooks are famous for their superb casseroles of meat, fish and poultry, enhanced with the subtle flavour of aromatic herbs and simmered gently in a sauce made rich with good stock, cream or wine. It is perhaps just this use of herbs and wines, and the words so often called on to describe these dishes – rich, unctuous, exotic, sophisticated – that have made the less adventurous cook too intimidated to attempt them.

For the uninitiated to whom cooking with wine may seem as extravagant as it is difficult, the well-known author and gourmet, Paul Gallico, set down this golden rule to dispel once and for all any misunderstanding: 'The only difference between cooking with wine and not cooking with wine is that you pour some wine in.'

My first contact with French food and wine was as dramatic and complete as any I have had since. It was in the winter of 1944, in the little river town of Duclair, just a few miles from Rouen. The dimly lit windows of a riverside inn beckoned the four travel-stained soldiers of the U.S. Army standing on the *quai*. We were young – not one of us over twenty-one – weary of the training, travel and camp life that were to prepare us for the push ahead, and hungry for food other than our army rations, for faces other than our camp companions, and for that something else which we all felt was waiting for us somewhere in this war-spoiled terrain of Northern France – the spirit of France itself.

This was to be our first meal in France, not perhaps as it should have been, but as the fortunes of war and of the pot would permit. The innkeeper, surprised to find soldiers asking for anything other than beer or Calvados, claimed at first that he had nothing to serve us. Then, taking pity on our youth and the fact that we had journeyed thousands of miles for this encounter, he disappeared for a moment or two into the cellars, to return with a slim white earthenware terrine and two dust-covered bottles – all that he could find to offer us – the *pâté* made for himself and his wife, and the wine hidden from the Germans behind bricked-over alcoves in the cellar.

The *pâté* was a home-made terrine of duck, its top covered with the rich golden-white fat of its own body, which had simmered slowly in the oven with a little wine to cover; the fillets of its breast and liver marbled the rich red-stained meat as we cut into it. Crusty bread and glasses of cellar-cooled claret completed this unforgettable meal, the perfect introduction to the pleasures of French food and wines, for *pâté de canard*, as made in Duclair, is one of the most famous dishes of Normandy, and Chantemerle, the wine he found for us that night, one of the noblest wines of all France.

Good food and wine have been the symbols of French living since they emerged together from the monasteries at the end of the Dark Ages. And they have been linked inextricably ever since.

Guardians of the pleasures of the tables as much as of the learning of the past, the monks kept the secrets of the gourmets safe for a thousand years after the Roman Empire collapsed. The kings of those days were merely chiefs; the barons taken up with wars. Not for them the finer points of the table.

But the traditions of good living persisted behind monastery walls. The strictest orders, though fasting themselves, provided hospitality for the great on pilgrimages or on their way to the wars, and for merchants traversing the ancient trade routes of Europe from the South to the Hanseatic Ports.

In their guests' refectories a more sophisticated cuisine persisted, and wine played its part in full. For as the great Cistercian and Benedictine monasteries cleared the wooded lands presented to them over the centuries, they planted them with vines. Some of the most famous vineyards in Burgundy – Clos Vougeot, for instance, belonged to the Abbey of Citeaux – were tended by monks forbidden by their order to drink the wines they produced. But they were not forbidden to sell them, and strategic gifts of their finest vintages to popes and kings often led to miraculous advancements for the clergy.

Equal miracles can be produced today by the marriage of the right wine with the right food. For the balance is important. In the districts where wine is grown and where cooking reaches its peak, a rustic cuisine accompanies the coarser wines; subtle cooking, the light wines; and rich full fare, the full-bodied vintages.

During the past few years there has been a revolution at our tables: the British are becoming a nation of wine drinkers. Not just for special occasions and holidays, but for everyday living. It is no longer the hallmark of the connoisseur to have a bottle of wine on the table. And the British housewife is catching up with her French counterpart, who has known this little kitchen secret all along: to make an everyday dish an event, just add a little wine.

The bouquet and flavour of a good table wine will vastly improve the quality of your cooking. Learn to cook with the same quality wines that you like to drink. There is no such thing as a good cooking wine; any wine that is fit to cook with is fit to drink. And a note to teetotallers . . . the cooking evaporates the alcohol in the wine and only the wonderful flavour remains.

Use wine to tenderise as well as flavour the type of dish that has made France famous – superb slow-cooking casseroles of meat, poultry and game, seized in a little butter or olive oil, enhanced with the flavour of aromatic herbs, and then simmered gently for hours in a sauce enriched with good stock and fine wine.

Let wine add flavour to soups, sauces, stews and salads. Lace a thick soup with dry sherry or Madeira; add a little dry white wine to a salad dressing for fish or potatoes; combine white wine with powdered saffron and a well-flavoured French dressing for a Spanish-style salad of fish and shellfish cooked in a *court-bouillon* of white wine and water, spiked with vinegar and flavoured with onion, carrots, lemon peel and bay leaf.

Louis Outhier, handsome young chef-proprietor of the Oasis restaurant in La Napoule, just along the coast from Cannes, who trained with the famous Fernand Point at Vienne, uses wine to advantage in his sauces. He is one of the best chefs along the Coast, and the hard-to-find Oasis – it is in a back street just off the coastal road – is one of the most rewarding stop-offs for discerning visitors. There you can enjoy the specialities of the chef – **loup de mer en croûte**, a freshly caught sea bass half cooked in a white wine *court-bouillon*, placed on a large board, its form, fins, tail, eyes and scales remodelled in *brioche* pastry, and baked until golden in the oven. This masterpiece is served at the table, letting out all its aroma as it is cut before your eyes. Louis Outhier's **lobster belle aurore** is lobster poached in a white wine *court-bouillon* flavoured with onion, carrot, tomato and cognac. The lobster is split, the meat removed from the shell, sliced and combined with the *court-bouillon*, reduced to a thick sauce and blended with equal parts of fresh cream and sauce Hollandaise. The whole is returned to the half-shell, sprinkled with freshly grated Parmesan and browned quickly under the grill.

Sauces with a red wine base can add distinctive savour to delicious hurry-up dishes too; try **ouefs en meurette,** poached eggs served on *croûtons* of fried bread and covered with a red wine sauce, or roast beef *à la bordelaise*, thin slices of rare roast beef simmered in butter and then bathed in a red wine sauce. Beefsteak *à la bordelaise* – rare beefsteak served with a red wine sauce – is a wonderful variation on the grilled meat theme. Even hamburgers and meat loaf are greatly improved by the addition of this simple sauce.

Seafood

10

Cod Steaks Baked with Saffron

1 Spanish onion, finely chopped
4 level tablespoons butter
4 level tablespoons fresh breadcrumbs
salt and freshly ground black pepper
2 tablespoons olive oil
4 medium-sized cod steaks
150 ml/¼ pint chicken stock
¼–½ level teaspoon saffron
150 ml/¼ pint dry white wine
juice of ½ lemon
2 level tablespoons finely chopped parsley

1. Sauté finely chopped onion in butter until onion is soft. Add breadcrumbs and cook for 5 minutes more. Season with salt and freshly ground black pepper. Remove onion and breadcrumb mixture with a slotted spoon and reserve.

2. Add olive oil to casserole; place cod steaks in casserole, season with salt and freshly ground black pepper and sauté for 3 minutes on each side. Spoon onion and breadcrumb mixture around steaks.

3. Heat chicken stock with saffron and pour over cod steaks. Pour over dry white wine, cover casserole, and cook in a moderate oven (180°C, 350°F, Gas Mark 4) for 20 minutes. Remove cover from casserole and continue to cook for 5 or 10 minutes longer. Just before serving, sprinkle cod steaks with lemon juice and finely chopped parsley.

Smoked Haddock Casserole

1 kg/2 lb smoked haddock
water and milk, to cover
butter
3 level tablespoons flour
450 ml/¾ pint cream
¼–½ level teaspoon turmeric
freshly ground black pepper
freshly grated nutmeg
2 level tablespoons finely chopped parsley
triangles of bread

1. Soak haddock in cold water for 2 hours. Drain haddock, put it in a saucepan and cover with equal amounts of water and milk. Bring to a fast boil. Remove from heat and allow to stand for 15 minutes. Drain haddock, reserving stock.

2. Melt 3 level tablespoons butter in the top of a double saucepan. Stir in flour and cook over water for 3 minutes, stirring continuously, until smooth. Add cream and enough turmeric (dissolved in a little hot water) to give a rich golden colour to the sauce. Continue to cook, stirring from time to time.

3. Boil 300 ml/½ pint haddock stock to reduce it to half its original quantity and add enough of this highly-flavoured stock to give savour to your sauce. Season to taste with freshly ground black pepper and a little grated nutmeg.

4. Remove skin and bones from haddock and break into large pieces. Arrange pieces in a shallow flameproof casserole, pour over sauce and simmer very gently until ready to serve.

5. Sprinkle with finely chopped parsley and serve in the casserole surrounded by triangles of bread which you have sautéed in butter.

Baked Plaice with Mushrooms

300 ml/½ pint milk
salt
8–12 fresh fillets of plaice
dried breadcrumbs
butter
dried tarragon
freshly ground black pepper
225 g/8 oz button mushrooms, thinly sliced
4 level tablespoons finely chopped shallots
4 tablespoons melted butter
juice of ½ lemon

1. Flavour milk with salt. Dip plaice fillets in the milk and then in the breadcrumbs. Set aside.

2. Butter an ovenproof shallow casserole. Lay prepared fillets in it and season with dried tarragon, salt and freshly ground black pepper, to taste.

3. Sauté thinly sliced mushrooms and finely chopped shallots in 4 tablespoons butter until vegetables begin to turn colour; scatter over fish. Dribble the melted butter and lemon juice over them and bake in a hot oven (220°C, 425°F, Gas Mark 7) until fish flakes easily with a fork.

Curried Plaice with Rice

8–12 fillets of plaice
butter
1 Spanish onion, finely chopped
1½ level tablespoons curry powder
salt and freshly ground black pepper
juice of ½ lemon
**300 ml/½ pint well-flavoured Béchamel
    Sauce (see page 91)**
**300 ml/½ pint dry white wine, reduced over
    a high heat to ⅓ the original quantity**
boiled rice to serve

1. Slice each fillet into 3 pieces.

2. Melt 2 tablespoons butter in a shallow flame-proof casserole; add finely chopped onion and sauté until transparent. Stir in 1 level tablespoon curry powder, and season to taste with salt and freshly ground black pepper.

3. Spread onion mixture over the bottom of casserole and arrange fish pieces on top. Dot with butter, cover casserole and cook for 10 minutes over a medium heat. Remove cover, sprinkle with remaining curry powder and lemon juice.

4. Flavour Béchamel Sauce with reduced white wine and pour over fish to cover it. Cover casserole and simmer over a low heat for 15 minutes. Serve with boiled rice.

12

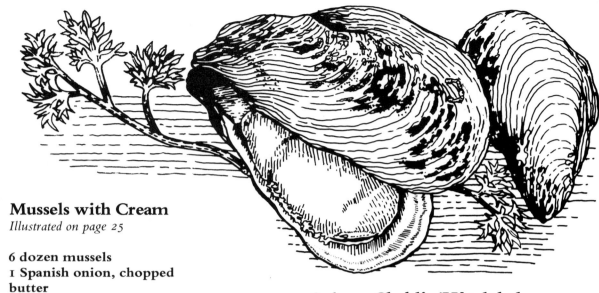

Mussels with Cream
Illustrated on page 25

6 dozen mussels
1 Spanish onion, chopped
butter
300 ml/½ pint dry white wine
2–3 sprigs parsley
1 sprig thyme
1 bay leaf
freshly ground black pepper
1 level tablespoon flour
6 level tablespoons double cream
2 level tablespoons chopped parsley

1. Scrape, beard and wash mussels thoroughly.

2. Sauté chopped onion in 2 level tablespoons butter in a large casserole until transparent but not coloured.

3. Add wine, parsley, thyme and bay leaf, and freshly ground black pepper, to taste, and simmer gently for 10 minutes. Add mussels to this mixture. Cover casserole and steam, shaking constantly, until mussel shells open.

4. Pour off cooking liquid into a small saucepan and reduce over a high heat to half the original quantity. Thicken sauce by adding a *beurre manié*, made by creaming together 2 tablespoons butter and 1 tablespoon flour. Cook over high heat, stirring constantly, until sauce is smooth. Add double cream, correct seasoning and pour sauce over mussels. Sprinkle with a little finely chopped parsley. Bring to the boil, remove from heat and serve immediately.

Sole au Chablis 'Hôtel de la Côte d'Or'

2 sole (about 450 g/1 lb each)
bones, head and trimmings from fish
150 ml/¼ pint water
salt and freshly ground black pepper
1 bouquet garni (1 bay leaf, 1 sprig thyme,
    4 sprigs parsley)
butter
2 shallots or small white onions, finely
    chopped
150 ml/¼ pint dry white Chablis

1. Ask your fishmonger to fillet the sole and give you the bones, head and trimmings to make a fish *fumet*. Simmer bones and trimmings for 15 minutes in water flavoured to taste with salt, freshly ground black pepper and a *bouquet garni*. Strain and reserve liquid.

2. Place fillets of sole in a well-buttered ovenproof *gratin* dish or shallow casserole. Sprinkle with finely chopped shallots (or onions) and add Chablis (or other dry white Burgundy), fish *fumet* and salt to taste. Cover with buttered paper and bake in a moderately hot oven (190°C, 375°F, Gas Mark 5) for about 15 minutes.

3. Arrange poached fillets on a heated serving dish; put fish liquor into a small saucepan and reduce over a high heat to half the original quantity. Whisk in 2 to 4 tablespoons butter, correct seasoning and strain sauce over sole. Serve immediately.

Turbot Baked in Cream

4 thick slices turbot
butter
salt and freshly ground black pepper
600 ml/1 pint double cream
lemon juice
Dijon mustard
Worcestershire sauce

1. Place turbot slices in a well-buttered ovenproof baking dish or shallow casserole, and season generously with salt and freshly ground black pepper.

2. Season cream to taste with lemon juice, Dijon mustard and Worcestershire sauce. Pour over fish and cover with buttered paper or a piece of foil. Place baking dish in a tin of boiling water in a moderately hot oven (190°C, 375°F, Gas Mark 5) for 15 to 20 minutes, until fish flakes easily with a fork.

3. To serve: transfer turbot to a heated serving dish, correct seasoning of sauce and strain over fish. Serve immediately.

Baked Fish with Mustard Sauce

1 white fish (1.5 kg/3 lb)
300 ml/½ pint dry white wine
150 ml/¼ pint water
2 tablespoons olive oil
4 level tablespoons finely chopped parsley
6 level tablespoons finely chopped shallots
2–3 level teaspoons dry mustard
salt and freshly ground black pepper

1. Clean and score fish and place in a baking dish.

2. Combine dry white wine, water, olive oil, finely chopped parsley and shallots with dry mustard that has been mixed with a little hot water.

Season to taste with salt and freshly ground black pepper, and pour liquid over fish.

3. Bake in a moderate oven (180°C, 350°F, Gas Mark 4) for 30 to 40 minutes, until the fish flakes easily at the touch of a fork, basting it every 10 minutes. Remove the fish to a heated serving platter, pour the basting sauce over the fish and serve.

Italian Fish Casserole

750 ml/1¼ pints well-flavoured chicken stock
225 g/8 oz long-grained rice
300 ml/½ pint well-flavoured Italian Tomato Sauce (see page 91)
675 g/1½ lb assorted fish, cut into pieces
butter
4 level tablespoons finely chopped parsley
salt and freshly ground black pepper
2 level tablespoons freshly grated Parmesan cheese
green salad to serve

1. Bring chicken stock to the boil, add rice and simmer until cooked through.

2. Prepare well-flavoured Tomato Sauce.

3. Remove any bones from the fish, add fish pieces to sauce and simmer until fish flakes easily with a fork.

4. Butter a shallow ovenproof *gratin* dish. Fill with rice mixed with finely chopped parsley. Season to taste with salt and freshly ground black pepper, and dot with knobs of butter. Arrange pieces of cooked fish on bed of rice, mask with sauce, sprinkle with grated cheese and put in a moderately hot oven (190°C, 375°F, Gas Mark 5) for 10 minutes. Serve with a green salad.

14

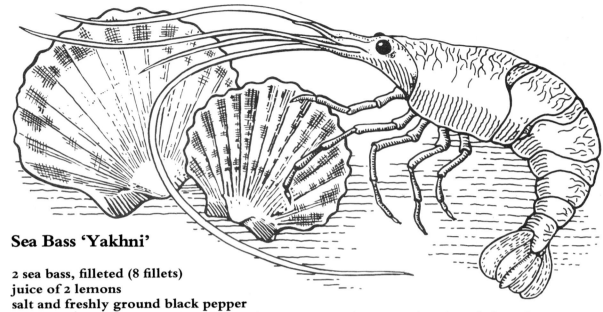

Sea Bass 'Yakhni'

2 sea bass, filleted (8 fillets)
juice of 2 lemons
salt and freshly ground black pepper
$\frac{1}{4}$ level teaspoon powdered cumin seed
Pilaff rice (see recipe below)

YAKHNI SAUCE
4 tablespoons olive oil
1 large Spanish onion, finely chopped
2 bay leaves
4-6 tablespoons finely chopped parsley
4 tablespoons finely chopped celery leaves
2 cloves garlic, finely chopped
450 g/1 lb tomatoes, peeled, seeded and
finely chopped
1 tablespoon tomato purée

1. Combine lemon juice, salt, freshly ground black pepper and powdered cumin in a bowl, and marinate fish fillets in the mixture for at least 1 hour, turning fillets occasionally.

2. To make Yakhni Sauce: heat oil in a shallow pan and sauté onion until transparent. Add bay leaves and finely chopped parsley, celery leaves and garlic, and simmer until vegetables begin to take on colour. Add tomatoes and tomato purée and simmer for 30 minutes longer, stirring from time to time.

3. To cook fish: 30 minutes before serving, spread half of the Yakhni Sauce over the bottom of a large ovenproof dish. Remove the fish fillets from the marinade juices, drain and arrange on the sauce. Pour over remaining sauce, cover with a piece of oiled paper and bake in a moderately hot oven (190°C, 375°F, Gas Mark 5) for 30 minutes, or until fish flakes with a fork. Serve hot with pilaff rice.

Pilaff Rice

350 g/12 oz long-grain rice
$\frac{1}{2}$ Spanish onion, finely chopped
butter
450 ml/$\frac{3}{4}$ pint well-flavoured stock
thyme
salt and freshly ground black pepper

1. Wash rice; drain and dry with a cloth.

2. Sauté finely chopped onion in 4 tablespoons butter until a light golden colour. Add rice and continue to cook, stirring constantly, until it begins to take on colour.

3. Pour in hot stock, and season to taste with thyme, salt and freshly ground black pepper. Cover pan and place in a moderate oven (180°C, 350°F, Gas Mark 4) for 15 to 20 minutes, until the liquid has been absorbed and the rice is tender but not mushy. Serve with additional butter.

Pot-au-feu de Poissons

**4 sticks celery, cut into 5-cm/2-inch
segments
4 carrots, cut into 5-cm/2-inch segments
4 leeks, cut into 5-cm/2-inch segments
butter
salt and freshly ground black pepper
600 ml/1 pint chicken stock
bones and trimmings from fish
575 g/1½ lb turbot fillets
575 g/1½ lb sole fillets
4-6 scallops
100 g/4 oz tiny Norwegian prawns
2 level tablespoons flour
300 ml/½ pint double cream
2 level tablespoons finely chopped parsley
2 level tablespoons finely chopped chives**

1. Cut celery, carrot and leek segments into thin
'matchstick' strips. Sauté vegetables in 2 level
tablespoons butter in a shallow flameproof casserole for a few minutes, season with salt and
freshly ground black pepper. Add half the chicken
stock and simmer until vegetables are just tender.
Remove vegetables from casserole with a slotted
spoon. Keep warm.

2. Add remaining chicken stock to casserole with
bones and trimmings from fish, season well with
salt and freshly ground black pepper and bring to
the boil. Skim, remove fish bones and trimmings
and poach turbot fillets in stock until fish flakes
with a fork. Remove and keep warm.

3. Add sole fillets to the casserole and poach for
several minutes until fish flakes with a fork.
Remove and keep warm.

4. Add scallops and prawns to the casserole and
poach for several minutes until scallops are cooked.
Remove scallops and prawns and keep warm.

5. Reduce cooking liquids over a high heat to one-
third of the original quantity.

6. In the meantime, melt 2 level tablespoons
butter in the top of a double saucepan over direct
heat. Add flour and cook, stirring constantly until
the *roux* is well blended. Then stir in reduced

fish stock and double cream and cook over simmering water, stirring from time to time, until
sauce is smooth and thick. Correct seasoning.

7. To assemble Pot-au-feu: divide the hot
seafood between 4 to 6 shallow bowls, arrange
poached vegetables decoratively among the serv-
ings, and top seafood and vegetables with the
sauce. Sprinkle each bowl with a little finely
chopped parsley and chives.

Brodet – a Red Fish Stew

**2 Spanish onions, thinly sliced
6 tablespoons olive oil
3 level tablespoons tomato purée
hot water
1.25 kg/2½ lb assorted fish, cut into pieces
300 ml/½ pint red wine
salt and freshly ground black pepper
100 g/4 oz cooked prawns
2 level tablespoons butter
4 level tablespoons finely chopped parsley
2 cloves garlic, finely chopped
grated rind of ½ lemon**

1. Sauté sliced onions in olive oil in a large flameproof casserole until onions are soft and transparent. Stir in tomato purée diluted in 4 tablespoons
hot water. Add fish pieces and continue to cook,
shaking casserole from time to time to keep fish
from sticking to bottom of casserole.

2. Add red wine to casserole and enough hot
water to just cover fish. Season generously with
salt and freshly ground black pepper and continue
to cook gently, shaking pan from time to time,
until fish flakes easily with a fork.

3. Sauté prawns in butter, finely chopped parsley
and garlic, and grated lemon rind. Sprinkle over
fish and serve immediately.

16

Mexican Fish Bake

1 kg/2 lb fish (cod, halibut, etc.)
butter
2 Spanish onions, sliced
6-8 tomatoes, thickly sliced
salt
paprika and cayenne
2 canned pimientos, cut in thin strips
300 ml/½ pint dry white wine
6-8 tablespoons olive oil

1. Clean fish and cut into pieces. Butter an oven-proof casserole generously and arrange fish, sliced onions and tomatoes in casserole in alternating layers – seasoning each layer with salt, paprika and cayenne, to taste.

2. Garnish the top layer with thin strips of pimiento and pour over wine and olive oil.

3. Bake fish and vegetables in a moderate oven (160°C, 325°F, Gas Mark 3) for 30 to 40 minutes, until fish flakes easily with a fork.

Egyptian Fish Taguen for One

2 tablespoons olive oil
1 small onion, finely chopped
1 small clove garlic, finely chopped
100 g/4 oz short-grain rice
1 fillet of sea bass, turbot or halibut,
  weighing about 175 g/6 oz
salt and freshly ground black pepper
300 ml/½ pint well-flavoured fish stock
1-2 Italian canned tomatoes, chopped
lemon slices

1. Heat the oil and add the onion and garlic. When the vegetables start to take on colour, add the rice and cook until it turns golden brown.

2. Place half the rice in a small earthenware casserole and top with fish. Season to taste with salt and freshly ground black pepper. Add remainder of rice and pour over all the fish stock and chopped tomato. Cook, covered, in a moderately hot oven (200°C, 400°F, Gas Mark 6) for 45 minutes to 1 hour. Serve garnished with lemon slices.

Prawn and Scallop Casserole

6 scallops
½ chicken stock cube
1 tablespoon lemon juice
350 g/12 oz prawns in their shells
dry white wine (optional)

SAUCE
butter
3 tablespoons flour
600 ml/1 pint hot milk
1 clove garlic, finely chopped
¼ level teaspoon dry mustard
1 level tablespoon tomato purée
freshly grated Gruyère cheese
salt and freshly ground black pepper
225 g/8 oz button mushrooms, quartered
2 level tablespoons finely chopped parsley

1. To make sauce: melt 3 tablespoons butter in the top of a double saucepan, stir in flour and cook over water, stirring constantly, until smooth. Add hot milk, stirring constantly, until well blended. Lower heat and simmer for 20 minutes. Then add finely chopped garlic, dry mustard, tomato purée, coarsely grated Gruyère and salt and freshly ground black pepper, to taste. Continue cooking, stirring constantly, until cheese melts.

2. Poach scallops for 10 minutes in just enough water to cover them to which you have added ½ chicken stock cube, lemon juice and salt and freshly ground black pepper, to taste. Drain, reserving liquid.

3. Poach prawns in their shells in remaining stock from scallops, adding more water (or water and dry white wine), to just cover prawns. Drain, reserving liquid.

4. To assemble casserole: peel prawns, slice scallops thinly and add prawns and sliced scallops to sauce. Sauté button mushrooms in 2 level tablespoons butter in a flameproof casserole. Strain 150 ml/¼ pint of liquid left from cooking shellfish into casserole and continue to simmer for 1 minute. Pour in prawns and scallops in sauce. Taste, correct seasoning and heat through. Garnish, just before serving, with chopped parsley.

Beef

Estouffade de Boeuf

1 large piece bacon rind, or fresh pork fat
1.5 kg/3½ lb lean beef
4 cloves garlic, cut into slivers
salt and freshly ground black pepper
1 bouquet garni (1 stick celery, 2 sprigs
  parsley, 2 sprigs thyme)
1 bay leaf
1 strip orange peel
225 g/8 oz green bacon, in 1 piece, diced
2 Spanish onions, halved
4 cloves
4 carrots, sliced lengthwise
8 shallots
4 tablespoons cognac
150 ml/¼ pint rich beef stock
good red wine

1. Lay a good-sized strip of bacon rind or fresh pork fat in the bottom of an ovenproof casserole. Stud meat with garlic slivers and rub with salt and freshly ground black pepper. Place on protective 'bed' of bacon rind and surround with *bouquet garni*, bay leaf, orange peel, diced green bacon, halved onions stuck with cloves, sliced carrots and shallots. Moisten with cognac and rich beef stock and add red wine until meat is practically covered.

2. Cover the casserole and cook in a moderately hot oven (190°C, 375°F, Gas Mark 5) for 1 hour. Reduce oven temperature to very cool (120°C, 250°F, Gas Mark ½) and cook until tender. Skim fat from sauce and remove *bouquet garni* before serving.

Pampas Beef with Olives

1.75 kg/4 lb lean beef
flour
5 tablespoons butter
4 tablespoons olive oil
salt and freshly ground black pepper
225 g/8 oz bacon, diced
2 cloves garlic
2 carrots, sliced
450 g/1 lb button onions
2 level tablespoons chopped parsley
2 bay leaves
2 sprigs thyme
1 small piece orange peel
1 bottle good red wine
12 ripe olives, stoned
12 mushrooms, sliced

1. Cut beef into large cubes, roll them in flour, and brown on all sides in 4 tablespoons butter and olive oil. Transfer to a casserole, and season to taste with salt and freshly ground black pepper.

2. Sauté diced bacon, garlic, carrots and onions in remaining fat until bacon is crisp and vegetables are golden. Transfer to casserole with meat. Add parsley, bay leaves, thyme and orange peel, and gradually moisten with 1 bottle of good red wine. Cook in a cool oven (150°C, 300°F, Gas Mark 2) for 1½ to 2 hours until meat is almost done.

3. Correct seasoning. Stir in, little by little, a *beurre manié* made with 1 level tablespoon flour blended to a paste with the same amount of butter. Add stoned ripe olives and sliced mushrooms, cover and allow to simmer in a cool oven or on the charcoal grill until mushrooms are cooked and meat is tender.

18

Boeuf en Daube

1.5 kg/3 lb lean top rump of beef
3 cloves garlic
100 g/4 oz fat salt pork
3 tablespoons olive oil
4 shallots, finely chopped
4 tomatoes, peeled, seeded and coarsely
   chopped
2 cloves garlic, finely chopped
12 button onions
100 g/4 oz button mushrooms, quartered
4 sprigs parsley
300 ml/½ pint rich beef stock
flour and water

MARINADE
3 slices lemon
1 bay leaf
pinch of thyme
1 level teaspoon finely chopped herbs
   (chives, tarragon, parsley)
150 ml/¼ pint dry white wine
1 tablespoon olive oil
salt and freshly ground black pepper

1. Make 6 small incisions in beef with a sharp knife and bury half a clove of garlic in each.

2. Combine ingredients of marinade mixture in a mixing bowl, and marinate meat in this mixture, turning occasionally, for 12 hours.

3. Remove rind from piece of fat salt pork. Dice pork and sauté in olive oil until golden. Remove pork bits, and brown beef well on all sides in the resulting amalgamation of fats.

4. Place pork rind in the bottom of an ovenproof casserole. Place beef on it and surround with sautéed pork bits, finely chopped shallots, peeled, seeded and coarsely chopped tomatoes, garlic, button onions, quartered button mushrooms and parsley. Strain the marinade juices over the meat and add beef stock.

5. Seal the casserole hermetically (make a thick paste of flour and water, shape it into a long, narrow roll and fit it round the edge of the casserole; press lid of casserole firmly into this

pastry band and seal). Cook in a very cool oven (120°C, 250°F, Gas Mark ½) for 4 to 5 hours. Serve from the casserole.

Beef Stew with Parsley Dumplings

1.5 kg/3½ lb stewing beef
flour
salt and freshly ground black pepper
2 level tablespoons butter or lard
2 tablespoons olive oil
hot water or beef stock (made with a stock
   cube)
12 button onions
12 small carrots
1 level tablespoon cornflour, dissolved in a
   little stock

PARSLEY DUMPLINGS
100 g/4 oz flour, sifted
2 level teaspoons baking powder
½ level teaspoon salt
2 level tablespoons butter
1 egg, beaten
2 level tablespoons finely chopped parsley
150 ml/¼ pint milk

1. Cut meat into 5-cm/2-inch cubes. Dredge in flour seasoned to taste with salt and freshly ground black pepper.

2. Heat fat and oil in a thick-bottomed flameproof casserole, and sauté meat until well browned on all sides. Add 600 ml/1 pint hot water or stock, cover casserole tightly and simmer gently for 1½ to 2 hours, until beef is tender. About 30 minutes before the end of cooking time, add onions and carrots, and more liquid if necessary.

3. Cover and continue to cook for 15 minutes. Drop parsley dumplings gently on top of stew, cover casserole and finish cooking.

4. To make parsley dumplings: combine sifted flour, baking powder and salt in a mixing bowl. Cut in butter with a pastry blender or with 2 knives. Combine beaten egg, parsley and milk, and stir into flour to make a soft dough. Scoop out dumpling mixture with a wet serving spoon,

19

and drop quickly by the spoonful on to meat and vegetables in casserole, leaving a little space at sides for steam to circulate. Cover casserole and steam gently for 15 minutes.

5. To serve: arrange meat, vegetables and dumplings on a heated serving dish and keep warm. Thicken gravy with cornflour which you have dissolved in a little stock.

Boeuf Sauté à la Bourguignonne 'Alexandre Dumaine'

1.25 kg/2½ lb beef
½ bottle red wine
225 g/8 oz carrots, sliced
25 g/1 oz shallots, finely chopped
50 g/2 oz onion, finely chopped
1–2 sprigs thyme
1–2 bay leaves
225 g/8 oz unsmoked bacon
12 button onions
12 baby carrots
1 level tablespoon flour
1 glass water
2–4 cloves garlic
1 bouquet garni (1 stick celery, 2 sprigs
**   thyme, 1 bay leaf, 2 sprigs parsley)**
salt and freshly ground black pepper
12 button mushrooms
butter

1. Cut beef into bite-sized pieces and marinate overnight in red wine with carrots, shallots, onion, thyme and bay leaves. Drain well.

2. Dice bacon and brown in a *cocotte* with small onions and carrots. When these are lightly coloured, remove them together with the bacon, and sauté drained beef in remaining fat until brown. Sprinkle with flour, and add red wine from marinade and a glass of water.

3. Return diced bacon, onions and carrots to the pan, and add garlic and a *bouquet garni*. Season to taste with salt and freshly ground black pepper. Simmer gently until meat is tender and the sauce reduced to half the original quantity – about 2¾ to 3 hours.

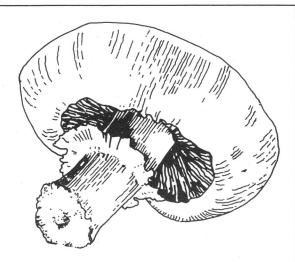

4. Brown mushrooms in butter and add to meat about 10 minutes before end of cooking.

Potted Tournedos

2 level tablespoons butter
4 thickly cut tournedos
6 shallots, finely chopped
French mustard
Worcestershire sauce
dried rosemary
salt and freshly ground black pepper
4 tablespoons cognac

1. Melt 1 level tablespoon butter in a frying pan and sauté tournedos (thick slices of fillet of beef, trimmed and tied with a thin strip of fat) for ½ to 1 minute on each side. Remove string and place in 4 individual ovenproof casseroles; keep warm.

2. Add remaining butter to pan and sauté finely chopped shallots until transparent. Add mustard and Worcestershire sauce, to taste, to the shallots; mix well and pour over tournedos.

3. Cover casseroles and cook for about 10 minutes in a hot oven (230°C, 450°F, Gas Mark 8). Drain off fat, turn tournedos over and add a pinch of rosemary, salt and freshly ground black pepper, to taste, to each casserole. Pour 1 tablespoon cognac over each tournedos and continue cooking for a few minutes longer. Serve in the casseroles.

Boeuf à l'Ail *Serves 6*
Flanders Carbonnade of Beef *Serves 4 to 6*
Stufatino di Manzo *Serves 4*

20

Boeuf à l'Ail

1.75 kg/4 lb beef (rump or top round)
4 level tablespoons butter
2 tablespoons olive oil
450 g/1 lb tomatoes, peeled, seeded and
**   chopped**
2–3 level tablespoons tomato purée
2 sprigs thyme
2 bay leaves
salt and freshly ground black pepper
4 cloves garlic
water, stock or dry white wine
noodles or boiled new potatoes to serve

1. Cut beef into cubes about 5 cm/2 inches square. Sauté cubes in butter and olive oil until well browned. Add tomatoes, tomato purée, thyme and bay leaves, and season to taste with salt and freshly ground black pepper.

2. Do not peel garlic; just smash cloves with the heel of your hand and add them to the casserole.

3. Simmer beef gently for about 3 hours, adding a little hot water, stock or white wine if meat becomes dry. Serve with noodles or new potatoes.

Flanders Carbonnade of Beef

1.25 kg/2½ lb beef (rump or round)
flour
225 g/8 oz green bacon
butter
olive oil
3 Spanish onions, sliced
150 ml/¼ pint boiling water
450 ml/¾ pint beer
2 level tablespoons finely chopped parsley
1 level teaspoon thyme
2 tablespoons wine vinegar
boiled potatoes to serve

1. Cut beef into 3.5-cm/1½-inch squares and flour lightly.

2. Dice green bacon and sauté gently in butter and olive oil in a large thick-bottomed frying pan. Transfer bacon to a large ovenproof casserole.

3. Sauté sliced onions in remaining fat until transparent and add to meats in casserole. Drain off fat, pour boiling water into frying pan and bring to the boil again, stirring in all the crusty bits from the sides of the pan. Pour over meat and vegetables.

4. Add beer, finely chopped parsley and thyme to casserole. Cover and cook in a cool oven (150°C, 300°F, Gas Mark 2) for about 2 hours. Just before serving, stir in wine vinegar. Serve with boiled potatoes.

Stufatino di Manzo

Illustrated on page 48

2 level tablespoons lard
2 level tablespoons olive oil
350 g/12 oz fat salt pork, cut into fingers
8 button mushrooms
8 button onions, poached until just tender
2 large Spanish onions, chopped
2 cloves garlic, chopped
4 level tablespoons flour
½ level teaspoon dried marjoram
salt and freshly ground black pepper
1.25 kg/2½ lb lean beef, cut into 3.5-cm/
**   1½-inch cubes**
150 ml/¼ pint red wine
4 level tablespoons tomato purée, diluted in
**   water**
1 strip orange peel

1. Melt lard and olive oil in a large, thick-bottomed pan or flameproof casserole. Add fingers of salt pork, button mushrooms and poached button onions, chopped onion and garlic, and sauté, stirring constantly, until golden. Remove salt pork and vegetables with a perforated spoon and reserve.

2. Combine flour and marjoram and salt and freshly ground black pepper, to taste, in a large bowl. Add meat and toss until cubes are coated with seasoned flour.

3. Add floured meat to casserole and cook, stirring frequently, until meat is well browned on all sides.

4. Now add red wine (one of the rougher Italian ones) and continue cooking until the wine is reduced to half the original quantity.

5. Add diluted tomato purée and strip orange peel. Cover casserole and simmer very gently for about 2 hours, or until the meat is tender and the sauce thick and richly coloured. Thirty minutes before serving add reserved bacon, aromatics and mushrooms and onions.

Note: A tablespoon or two of red wine just before serving will add extra *bouquet* to this dish.

Beef Marinated in Beer

1.75 kg/4 lb beef (rump or round)
4 tablespoons olive oil
2 level tablespoons brown sugar
2 level tablespoons flour
4 tablespoons red wine
4 level tablespoons double cream

BEER MARINADE
1 bottle beer (pale or brown ale)
600 ml/1 pint water
4 tablespoons olive oil
1 Spanish onion, sliced
6 carrots, sliced
2 bay leaves
6 peppercorns
2 cloves
1 level teaspoon allspice
salt

1. To make beer marinade: combine beer, water, olive oil, sliced onion and carrots, bay leaves and seasonings in a large mixing bowl.

2. Place beef in this marinade and marinate in the refrigerator for 2 or 3 days, turning meat once or twice each day.

3. When ready to cook: remove meat from marinade and drain, reserving marinade. Heat olive oil in a flameproof casserole just large enough to hold beef. Add meat, and brown on all sides. Pour 300 ml/½ pint marinade juices with vegetables and seasonings over meat. Cover cas-

serole and cook for 1¾ hours in a cool oven (150°C, 300°F, Gas Mark 2), adding more marinade juices during cooking if necessary.

4. Remove casserole from oven. Sprinkle meat with brown sugar and simmer on top of the cooker, uncovered, for 15 minutes longer, turning meat until sugar has melted and browned.

5. Stir flour into remaining marinade juices. Add red wine and pour over meat. Return casserole to oven, uncovered, for 30 minutes, or until sauce has thickened. Remove meat to a serving dish. Strain sauce and skim off any fat. Stir in double cream and pour over meat. Serve immediately.

Magyar Slow-cooked Beef Casserole

225 g/8 oz dried red beans
100 g/4 oz rice
1.25 kg/2½ lb beef, cut into 3.5-cm/1½-inch cubes
lard
salt and freshly ground black pepper
2 bay leaves
3 large tomatoes, cut in quarters
3 Spanish onions, thinly sliced
3 large carrots, thinly sliced
2 cloves garlic, chopped

1. Soak dried red beans overnight in cold water. Drain. Cook rice and beans in boiling salted water for 8 minutes. Drain.

2. Sauté beef in 4 level tablespoons lard until golden on all sides. Season generously with salt and freshly ground black pepper.

3. Place beef in a large flameproof casserole with partially cooked beans, bay leaves, quartered tomatoes, thinly sliced onions and carrots, chopped garlic and partially cooked rice. Add enough water to cover generously and bring liquid gently to the boil on top of the cooker. Skim.

4. Cover casserole and cook in a cool oven (150°C, 300°F, Gas Mark 2) for at least 3 hours, or until meat and vegetables are meltingly tender.

22

Yankee Pot Roast

1.75–2.75 kg/4–6 lb lean brisket of beef,
 in 1 piece
2 level tablespoons lard
2 tablespoons olive oil
600 ml/1 pint well-flavoured beef stock
4 large or 8 small carrots, quartered
2 Spanish onions, quartered
1 large or 2 small turnips, quartered
4 whole cloves
2 whole allspice
2 bay leaves
salt and freshly ground black pepper
freshly grated nutmeg

GARNISH
12 small carrots
12 small onions
3 large or 6 small turnips, quartered
stock or stock and water
6 potatoes

1. Brown beef well on all sides in lard and olive oil in a thick-bottomed flameproof casserole. Pour beef stock into the casserole and bring to the boil. Skim, then reduce heat. Add carrots, onions, turnip, cloves, allspice, bay leaves and salt, freshly ground black pepper and freshly grated nutmeg, to taste. Cook very gently for 2½ to 3 hours, until the meat is tender, making sure that the liquid barely simmers (to avoid the meat becoming tough) and only turning roast once during the cooking time.

2. Transfer meat to a heated serving dish and keep warm.

3. Thirty minutes before serving time, prepare the garnish. Poach prepared small carrots and onions and quartered turnips in a little stock, or stock and water, until just tender. Boil potatoes.

4. Garnish meat with freshly boiled vegetables.

5. Skim fat from sauce in casserole. Strain sauce into a small saucepan, thicken if desired and season with salt and freshly ground black pepper and nutmeg, to taste. Reheat and serve with meat and vegetables.

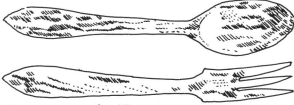

Carne Assada (Portuguese Pot Roast)

Illustrated on page 47

1.75 kg/4 lb rolled beef (round or rump), in
 1 piece
450 ml/¾ pint red wine
juice of ½ lemon
6 tablespoons olive oil
2 cloves garlic, finely chopped
1 level teaspoon salt
1 level teaspoon paprika
½ level teaspoon freshly ground black
 pepper
2 bay leaves
2 cloves
1 level tablespoon flour

GARNISH
fried potatoes
asparagus tips
halved hard-boiled eggs

1. Marinate beef overnight in red wine, lemon juice and 2 tablespoons olive oil, flavoured with garlic, salt, paprika, freshly ground black pepper, bay leaves and cloves.

2. Drain, reserving the juices. Brown meat in a flameproof casserole in the remaining olive oil. Add marinade juices. Cover casserole and cook in a moderate oven (160°C, 325°F, Gas Mark 3) for 2½ hours. Uncover casserole, baste meat with pan juices and continue to cook until meat is tender – about 30 minutes.

3. **To serve:** remove beef to a heated serving dish and keep warm. Thicken pan juices with flour, correct seasoning and strain. Arrange fried potatoes, cooked asparagus tips and halved hard-boiled eggs around carved meat. Pour a little sauce over meat and asparagus tips and serve remaining sauce separately.

Beef Vindaloo

2 Spanish onions, finely chopped
2 cloves garlic, finely chopped
olive oil
1 level tablespoon ground coriander seed
1 level teaspoon ground turmeric
1 level teaspoon freshly ground black pepper
$\frac{1}{2}$ level teaspoon powdered mustard
$\frac{1}{2}$ level teaspoon ground cumin seed
$\frac{1}{4}$ level teaspoon ground red pepper
$\frac{1}{4}$ level teaspoon ground ginger
grated peel and juice of $\frac{1}{2}$ lemon
1.25 kg/$2\frac{1}{2}$ lb shin of beef
flour
600 ml/1 pint light beef stock (made with a stock cube)
salt
rice to serve

1. Sauté finely chopped onions and garlic in 4 tablespoons olive oil in a flameproof casserole until onion is transparent. Add spices and lemon peel and juice and simmer, stirring constantly, for 2 to 3 minutes.

2. Cut beef into 2.5-cm/1-inch cubes, dust lightly with flour and add to lemon spice mixture. Stir well and cook for 10 minutes, adding a little more olive oil if necessary. Then add beef stock and salt to taste, cover casserole and simmer gently until beef is tender. Serve with rice.

Boeuf à la Corse 'Chez Victor, aux Deux Marches'

1.25 kg/$2\frac{1}{2}$ lb lean beef
$\frac{1}{2}$ calf's foot
225 g/8 oz unsmoked bacon, in 1 piece
2 tablespoons olive oil
2 level tablespoons butter
2 tablespoons cognac
2-3 level tablespoons tomato purée
1 Spanish onion, quartered
2 cloves garlic
1 bouquet garni (2 sprigs parsley, 2 sprigs thyme, 1 bay leaf, 1 stick celery)
salt and freshly ground black pepper
1 bottle red wine
125 g/$4\frac{1}{2}$ oz dried mushrooms
75-100 g/3-4 oz green olives, stoned
2-3 level tablespoons finely chopped parsley

1. Cut beef into cubes about 5 cm/2 inches square.

2. Put calf's foot and bacon in a pan of cold water and bring to the boil. Drain and dry well.

3. Heat olive oil and butter in a large thick-bottomed flameproof casserole. Add beef, calf's foot and bacon, and sauté until meats are golden brown. Add cognac, and flame. Then add tomato purée, onion, garlic and *bouquet garni*, and season to taste with salt and freshly ground black pepper. Add just enough red wine to cover the meat. Cover casserole and simmer gently for $1\frac{1}{2}$ hours, adding hot water occasionally if necessary.

4. Then add dried mushrooms, which have been soaked for 30 minutes in warm water, and stoned olives. Continue to cook for 15 minutes.

5. Remove *bouquet garni*, sprinkle with finely chopped parsley and serve in the casserole.

24

Hochepot de Queue de Boeuf

1 large oxtail
225 g/8 oz butter
4 medium-sized onions, sliced
3 large carrots, sliced
3 cloves garlic, crushed
1 glass good brandy
1 bottle Chablis
600 ml/1 pint rich beef stock
salt and freshly ground black pepper
1 bouquet garni (2 sprigs parsley, 2 sprigs
   thyme, 2 bay leaves, 1 stick celery)
24 button mushrooms
100 g/4 oz fat salt pork, diced
24 tiny onions
sugar
finely chopped parsley
purée of peas or chestnuts

1. Cut large oxtail into 10-cm/4-inch segments and blanch in cold water for at least 6 hours. Drain well and dry lightly with a clean towel.

2. Melt 4 tablespoons butter in a large thick-bottomed saucepan or flameproof casserole, and sauté the pieces of oxtail with sliced onions and carrots until golden. Then add crushed garlic. Cover casserole for 2 minutes, pour in brandy, and flame. Put out the flames with a bottle of dry Chablis. Add just enough rich beef stock to cover the pieces of oxtail. Add salt, freshly ground black pepper, and a *bouquet garni*, and simmer for 3 hours.

3. Strain sauce into a bowl through a fine sieve.

4. Place pieces of oxtail in a clean casserole and garnish with mushrooms which you have sautéed lightly in 2 tablespoons butter, diced fat salt pork which you have sautéed in 2 tablespoons butter, and onions which you have simmered until tender in a little water with the remaining butter and a little sugar.

5. Skim fat from surface of sauce, then pour sauce over the meat and vegetables. Bring slowly to the boil, cover the casserole and cook in a moderate oven (160°C, 325°F, Gas Mark 3) for 1 hour. When the *hochepot* is done, the meat should be meltingly tender and the sauce rich and smooth, and slightly thick without the aid of flour or a *beurre manié*.

6. Sprinkle with chopped parsley and serve from the casserole with a purée of peas or chestnuts.

Chili con Carne with Red Wine

1 kg/2 lb minced lean beef
1 Spanish onion, finely chopped
2 cloves garlic, chopped
2–3 level tablespoons bacon fat
1 (425-g/15-oz) can Italian peeled tomatoes
300 ml/$\frac{1}{2}$ pint red wine
3 level tablespoons Mexican chili powder*
1 level tablespoon flour
2 bay leaves, crumbled
$\frac{1}{4}$ level teaspoon powdered cumin
$\frac{1}{2}$ level teaspoon oregano
salt and freshly ground black pepper
2 (432-g/15$\frac{1}{4}$-oz) cans red kidney beans,
   drained
boiled rice to serve

*Note: Spice Islands brand or Twin Trees or McCormicks – not powdered chillies.

1. Sauté minced meat, chopped onion and chopped garlic in bacon fat until brown in a thick-bottomed flameproof casserole.

2. Add Italian canned tomatoes (with their juice) and red wine; bring again to the boil. Skim, cover casserole and simmer very gently for about 1 hour.

3. Blend chili powder with flour in a little of the hot pan juices and add to the casserole at the same time as crumbled bay leaves, cumin, oregano and salt and freshly ground black pepper, to taste.

4. Simmer over a low heat until meat is tender. Check seasoning; add canned red kidney beans and heat through. Serve with boiled rice.

Mexican Beans (see page 58)

Boston Baked Beans (see page 57)

Aubergine and Minced Lamb Casserole (see page 54)

Lamb

Daube de Mouton

1 leg of lamb
225 g/8 oz bacon, thinly sliced, and
   225 g/8 oz bacon, in 1 piece
olive oil
salt and freshly ground black pepper
dried thyme
marjoram
crumbled bay leaves
4-6 level tablespoons finely chopped onion
1 bouquet garni (2 sprigs parsley, 2 sprigs
   thyme, 1 stick celery, 1 bay leaf)
1 strip dried orange peel
well-flavoured stock
flour and water paste

MARINADE
red wine
4 tablespoons olive oil
2 carrots, finely chopped
1 Spanish onion, finely chopped
4 cloves garlic, smashed
1 bay leaf
2 sprigs thyme
1 sprig rosemary
4 sprigs parsley
salt and freshly ground black pepper

1. Bone leg of lamb and cut it into large pieces weighing about 75 g/3 oz each.

2. Cut half the bacon slices into 5-mm/¼-inch strips. Lard each of the lamb pieces with 2 strips of bacon which you have rubbed with a little olive oil, salt, freshly ground black pepper, dried thyme, marjoram and crumbled bay leaf.

Note: If you do not have a larding needle, cut 2 holes in meat cubes with a thin-bladed knife and insert strips of well-seasoned bacon into holes with the point of a skewer.

3. **To marinate meat:** place prepared lamb cubes in a large earthenware bowl and add just enough red wine to cover meat. Add 4 tablespoons olive oil, finely chopped carrots and Spanish onion, garlic, bay leaf, thyme, rosemary and parsley, and salt and freshly ground black pepper, to taste. Marinate for at least 4 hours.

4. **To cook daube:** dice uncut bacon and blanch it with remaining bacon slices. Cover the bottom of a large earthenware ovenproof casserole with a layer of lamb cubes. Sprinkle with 4 tablespoons finely chopped onion and half the diced blanched bacon, and season with a pinch of dried thyme and crumbled bay leaf. Cover with a layer of lamb and sprinkle with onions, bacon and dried herbs as above. Drop in a *bouquet garni* and a strip of dried orange peel. Then cover with a final layer of lamb cubes right to the very top of the casserole. Pour in strained marinade juices and a little stock. Top with remaining thin bacon slices, cover casserole and wrap a band of paste (made with flour and water) around join to seal it completely. Cook for 2½ to 3 hours in a cool oven (150°C, 300°F, Gas Mark 2).

5. **To serve:** remove pastry seal and the cover then remove bacon strips and *bouquet garni*. Skim and serve *daube* from casserole.

Lamb en Cocotte

1 loin of lamb, boned and rolled
thin strips of bacon
2 level tablespoons butter
2 tablespoons olive oil
2 large carrots, sliced
2 Spanish onions, sliced
salt and freshly ground black pepper
1 glass dry white wine or water
2-4 tomatoes, quartered

1. Lard rolled loin of lamb with thin strips of bacon.

2. Melt butter and olive oil in a thick-bottomed *cocotte* or casserole just large enough to hold lamb and add sliced carrots and onions. Simmer, stirring, until onion is transparent. Add meat and season to taste with salt and freshly ground black pepper. Sauté lamb until golden on all sides.

3. Transfer casserole to a moderate oven (160°C, 325°F, Gas Mark 3) and cook, uncovered, for 1½ to 2 hours, until lamb is tender, adding a little dry white wine or hot water if necessary to prevent *cocotte* from scorching. When meat is half cooked, add quartered tomatoes.

30

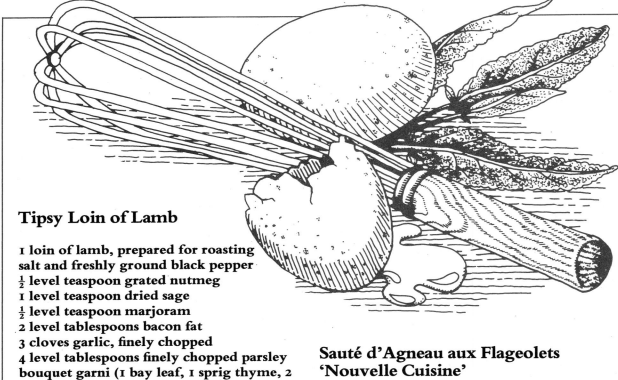

Tipsy Loin of Lamb

1 loin of lamb, prepared for roasting
salt and freshly ground black pepper
½ level teaspoon grated nutmeg
1 level teaspoon dried sage
½ level teaspoon marjoram
2 level tablespoons bacon fat
3 cloves garlic, finely chopped
4 level tablespoons finely chopped parsley
bouquet garni (1 bay leaf, 1 sprig thyme, 2
**   sprigs green celery leaves)**
claret
450 ml/¾ pint beef stock
1 level tablespoon flour
1 level tablespoon butter

1. Rub lamb well on all sides with salt and freshly ground black pepper, nutmeg, sage and marjoram.

2. Sear meat in hot bacon fat with finely chopped garlic and parsley. Place roast in a flameproof oval casserole. Add *bouquet garni*, tied with heavy white thread. Cover meat with claret and cook uncovered in a moderately hot oven (190°C, 375°F, Gas Mark 5), allowing 30 to 35 minutes per half kilo/per lb. Turn meat occasionally. When meat is done, the wine will have evaporated.

3. Remove meat and keep warm. Pour beef stock into casserole with pan juices, and reduce over a high heat to half the original quantity.

4. Brown flour in butter and mix with a little stock until smooth. Stir this *roux* into remaining stock and cook, stirring constantly, until sauce is thick and smooth. Correct seasoning and serve with meat.

Sauté d'Agneau aux Flageolets 'Nouvelle Cuisine'

1 rack of lamb, trimmed
salt and freshly ground black pepper
1 bay leaf
olive oil
1 (340-g/12-oz) can flageolets
butter
2 level tablespoons finely chopped parsley or
**   chives**

SAUCE
bones and trimmings from rack of lamb
½ chicken stock cube
2 level tablespoons tomato purée
½ Spanish onion, finely chopped
1 bay leaf
4 tablespoons dry white wine
1 level teaspoon flour
1 level teaspoon butter
freshly ground black pepper
salt

1. Cut meat from bones of lamb, making a 'fillet' of lamb. Cut the 'fillet' into 2.5-cm/1-inch thick slices. Trim each slice into three or four even-sized cubes, according to size of lamb. Reserve bones and meat trimmings and scraps for sauce.

2. Season lamb cubes generously with salt and freshly ground black pepper, add bay leaf and 4 level tablespoons olive oil. Toss well and leave lamb to marinate for at least 2 hours.

3. **To make sauce:** chop lamb bones coarsely and place in a thick-bottomed saucepan, or small flameproof casserole, with the lamb trimmings, ½ chicken stock cube, tomato purée, finely chopped onion, bay leaf and wine. Add water to just cover and simmer gently until meat on bones is cooked through. Strain stock into clean saucepan and cook over a high heat until it is reduced to half its original quantity. Whisk in *beurre manié*, made by mashing 1 level teaspoon each flour and butter to a smooth paste. Season with freshly ground black pepper, and salt. Keep warm.

4. **When ready to cook lamb:** drain canned *flageolets*, season with salt and freshly ground black pepper and sauté for a few minutes in butter. Sear lamb in oil on all sides until golden brown but still quite rare. Pour off excess fats, add sauce and then add *flageolets* and bring to the bubble. Sprinkle with finely chopped parsley or chives and serve immediately.

Lamb Blanquette with Ham

Illustrated on page 48

1 kg/2 lb boned shoulder or leg of lamb
225 g/8 oz cooked ham, in 1 piece
2 tablespoons olive oil
12 button onions
1 bouquet garni (2 sprigs parsley, 1 stick
   celery, 2 bay leaves, 2 sprigs thyme)
600 ml/1 pint boiling water or light stock
salt and freshly ground black pepper
4 level tablespoons butter
12 button mushrooms
2 level tablespoons flour
2 egg yolks
150 ml/¼ pint cream
juice of ½ lemon

1. Cut lamb and ham into cubes and place in a flameproof casserole. Sauté in olive oil until golden. Add onions and stir for 2 minutes. Then add the *bouquet garni*. Add boiling water or light stock, season generously and reduce heat until liquid barely simmers. Cover casserole and simmer for 1 to 1½ hours until meat is tender.

2. Drain cooking stock into a bowl; discard *bouquet garni* and place meat in a clean casserole to keep warm.

3. Melt 2 level tablespoons butter in a small pan and sauté mushrooms for 5 minutes, stirring occasionally. Add to the meat.

4. Make a *roux* with 2 level tablespoons butter and 2 level tablespoons flour in the top of a double saucepan. Add strained stock and stir over water until sauce is smooth and thick. Remove from heat.

5. Blend egg yolks, cream and lemon juice and 'finish' sauce by adding a quarter of the hot stock to egg and cream mixture. Pour this mixture into remaining stock and heat through until thick. Add salt and freshly ground black pepper if desired. Strain sauce through a fine sieve over the meat, heat through and serve immediately.

Irish Stew

1.5 kg/3 lb shoulder of mutton
450 g/1 lb onions
1 kg/2 lb potatoes
salt and freshly ground black pepper
light stock
3 level tablespoons chopped parsley

1. Cut mutton in 6-cm/2½-inch cubes; peel and slice onions thinly. Peel and slice potatoes thickly.

2. Place a layer of sliced onions on the bottom of a flameproof casserole. Cover with a layer of meat, then a layer of potatoes, and continue filling casserole in alternate layers, finishing with potatoes. Season each layer with salt and freshly ground black pepper. Add light stock, to cover. Bring to the boil, skim and lower heat. Simmer very gently, covered, until tender – almost 3 hours.

3. Just before serving, sprinkle with chopped parsley.

32

Shoulder of Lamb Camarguaise

1 shoulder of lamb
salt and freshly ground black pepper
butter
olive oil
well-flavoured stock
2–3 level tablespoons tomato purée
mushroom stalks
bouquet garni (2 sprigs parsley, 2 sprigs
   thyme, 1 bay leaf)

MARINADE
3 tablespoons olive oil
450 ml/¾ pint dry white wine
2 Spanish onions, chopped
4 large carrots, chopped
2 cloves garlic, smashed

RISOTTO STUFFING
225 g/8 oz short-grain rice
salt
1 canned pimiento, cut in thin strips
6 black olives, stoned and cut in strips
6 button mushroom caps, thinly sliced
3 level tablespoons butter
freshly grated Gruyère cheese
freshly ground black pepper

1. Ask your butcher to bone lamb; do not let him tie it. Ask for bones. Season boned shoulder of lamb generously with salt and freshly ground black pepper. Place lamb in a porcelain or earthenware casserole with marinade ingredients. Marinate lamb in this mixture for at least 8 hours, turning meat from time to time.

2. To make risotto stuffing: cook short-grain rice in boiling salted water until it is tender but not mushy. Drain well. Simmer strips of pimiento, olives and mushrooms in butter until soft. Combine with rice and season to taste with freshly grated Gruyère, salt and freshly ground black pepper.

3. To stuff lamb: drain lamb, reserving vegetables and juices of marinade. Wipe lamb dry and lay out on a table. Season with salt and freshly ground black pepper, and lay risotto stuffing down centre of meat. Tie up meat.

4. Brown lamb well on all sides in butter and olive oil. Place it in a flameproof casserole with bones and the vegetables of the marinade. Add marinade juices and well-flavoured stock to cover lamb. Stir in tomato purée, mushroom stalks and *bouquet garni*. Bring to the boil, lower heat and cover casserole. Simmer lamb gently for 2 hours.

5. Remove lamb from casserole and keep warm. Bring stock to the boil and cook until reduced to half the original quantity. Strain through a fine sieve. Thicken if necessary with a little *beurre manié*, made by mashing together equal quantities of flour and butter, and keep warm.

6. To serve: remove strings from lamb and place it on a heated serving dish. Pour a little sauce over lamb and serve immediately with the remaining sauce in a sauceboat.

Turkish Lamb Casserole with Green Beans

1 Spanish onion, finely chopped
2 level tablespoons butter
4 tablespoons olive oil
1.25 kg/2½ lb lamb, cut from leg
flour
salt and freshly ground black pepper
6 tomatoes, peeled, seeded and coarsely
   chopped
600 ml/1 pint chicken stock (made with a
   stock cube)
450 g/1 lb green beans
juice of ½ lemon (optional)

1. Sauté finely chopped onion in butter and olive oil in a flameproof casserole until onion is transparent.

2. Cut meat into even-sized cubes; roll in seasoned flour and add to onion. Simmer gently, stirring from time to time, until meat absorbs onion juices.

3. Add chopped tomatoes and chicken stock. Cover casserole and simmer gently over a low heat for 30 minutes.

4. Slice green beans into 2.5-cm/1-inch segments and add to casserole. Cover casserole again and continue to cook, over a moderate flame, until beans are tender. Correct seasoning, adding lemon juice, and salt and freshly ground black pepper, if desired.

Braised Stuffed Shoulder of Lamb

1 shoulder of lamb
olive oil
salt and freshly ground black pepper
lemon juice
flour
butter
beef, veal or chicken stock, or dry white
   wine
½ calf's foot (optional)

STUFFING
225 g/8 oz sausagemeat
½ Spanish onion, finely chopped and sautéed
   in butter
2 level tablespoons butter
2 level tablespoons finely chopped parsley
1 egg, beaten
225 g/8 oz spinach, chopped and sautéed in
   butter
salt and freshly ground black pepper
cumin or coriander

1. Ask your butcher to bone and trim a shoulder of lamb ready for rolling. Do not let him roll this.

2. Brush lamb with olive oil, and season to taste with salt and freshly ground black pepper. Sprinkle with lemon juice.

3. To make stuffing: in a large mixing bowl combine sausagemeat, finely chopped onion

which you have sautéed in butter until transparent, finely chopped parsley, beaten egg, sautéed spinach, and salt, freshly ground black pepper and spices to taste. Mix well.

4. Lay this stuffing on meat; roll up and sew up with fine string. Dust the lamb with flour and brown meat slowly on all sides in equal quantities of olive oil and butter in an oval *cocotte* or flameproof casserole just large enough to hold it.

5. Moisten the lamb with a little hot stock (beef, veal or chicken), dry white wine, or even hot water. Cover casserole, lower heat and cook for $1\frac{1}{2}$ to 2 hours, adding a little more liquid from time to time if necessary.

Note: If thicker sauce is desired, add half a calf's foot after meat is browned.

Lamb Stew with Courgettes

1.25 kg/2½ lb boned shoulder of lamb
4 tablespoons olive oil
1 Spanish onion, finely chopped
1 (793-g/1 lb 12-oz) can Italian peeled
   tomatoes
2–4 level tablespoons tomato purée, diluted
   in water
2–4 level tablespoons finely chopped parsley
oregano
salt and freshly ground black pepper
1 kg/2 lb courgettes
4 level tablespoons butter

1. Cut lamb into 5-cm/2-inch cubes. Heat oil in a thick-bottomed flameproof casserole and brown lamb on all sides. Add chopped onion and cook until lightly browned.

2. Add tomatoes and diluted tomato purée and season to taste with chopped parsley, oregano, salt and freshly ground black pepper. Bring to the boil, reduce heat and cover casserole. Simmer gently for 1 hour.

3. Brown courgettes in butter, add them to the casserole and continue cooking for 30 minutes longer, or until meat and vegetables are cooked.

34

Old Fashioned Mutton Stew

This mutton stew is prepared in a special way. The boned neck of mutton is particularly suitable for stews because it is juicy and gelatinous.

1 kg/2 lb boned shoulder of mutton
1 kg/2 lb boned breast or neck of mutton
3 Spanish onions, thinly sliced
6 large baking potatoes, peeled and sliced
1 bouquet garni (2 sprigs parsley, 2 sprigs thyme, 1 stick celery, 1 bay leaf)
salt and freshly ground black pepper
4 leeks, thinly sliced
16 small potatoes, pared into regular oval shapes
16 small white onions, blanched
butter
4 level tablespoons freshly chopped parsley
Worcestershire sauce to serve

1. Cut meat into squares 100–150 g/4–5 oz each. In order to keep mutton white, soak in cold water for a few hours or blanch just before making stew.

To blanch mutton: put meat in a large pan and add water to cover. Bring to the boil, drain immediately, refresh with cold water and drain again.

2. Arrange alternate layers of meat, sliced onions and sliced potatoes in a large flameproof casserole. Add *bouquet garni* and season to taste with salt and freshly ground black pepper. Top with thinly sliced leeks.

3. Add just enough water to cover. Cover casserole and simmer for about 1½ hours or until meat is tender. Then remove meat from casserole and add small potatoes and small onions. Add more water, if necessary, and correct seasoning. Cover casserole with a piece of buttered paper and then cover with lid. Simmer for 20 to 30 minutes, until vegetables are cooked. Return meat to casserole and heat through. Sprinkle with chopped parsley just before serving. Serve in the casserole, accompanied with Worcestershire sauce.

Note: The starchy baking potatoes, onions and leeks should disintegrate to a flavoursome sauce.

Navarin de Mouton aux Aromates

1.5 kg/3 lb boned shoulder or breast of lamb, or a combination of the two
2 level tablespoons butter
2 tablespoons olive oil
2 Spanish onions, quartered
2 level tablespoons flour
granulated sugar
salt and freshly ground black pepper
4 small turnips, quartered
1 bouquet garni (2 sprigs parsley, 2 sprigs thyme, 1 bay leaf)
300 ml/½ pint light stock
4 level tablespoons tomato purée, diluted in water
12 small white onions
100 g/4 oz unsmoked bacon, diced
12 small potatoes, peeled
100 g/4 oz fresh peas
4 anchovy fillets, finely chopped
4 tablespoons finely chopped parsley
2 large cloves garlic, finely chopped
grated rind of 1 lemon

1. Cut lamb into cubes and brown in butter and olive oil with quartered onions.

2. Remove some of the fat; blend in flour, stirring over low heat until slightly thickened. Sprinkle with a generous pinch or two of granulated sugar to give a deeper colour to the sauce, and season to taste with salt and freshly ground black pepper.

3. Add quartered turnips and *bouquet garni*. Stir in stock and diluted tomato purée. Simmer, covered, in a moderate oven (180°C, 350°F, Gas Mark 4) for 1 hour.

4. Drain the pieces of lamb in a sieve, reserving sauce, and remove bits of skin and bones which have separated from meat during cooking.

5. Allow sauce to cool; skim off fat, and strain the sauce into a clean casserole. Add pieces of lamb. Then glaze button onions, blanch and sauté diced unsmoked bacon, peel potatoes, shell peas, and add all these to the stew. Bring to the boil and cook, covered, in a moderate oven for 30 to 40 minutes, until vegetables are cooked and lamb is tender. Correct seasoning and sprinkle with finely chopped anchovies, parsley, garlic and grated lemon rind. Serve from casserole.

Lamb Curry with Yogurt

1.25 kg/2½ lb boned shoulder of lamb, cut into 6-cm/2½-inch cubes
2 level tablespoons butter
2 tablespoons olive oil
2 Spanish onions, chopped
2 cloves garlic, finely chopped
300 ml/½ pint yogurt
1 level tablespoon curry powder
¼ level teaspoon each ginger and turmeric
⅛ level teaspoon each paprika and cayenne
1 level tablespoon flour
sea salt and freshly ground black pepper
light stock (optional)

1. Heat butter and olive oil in a thick-bottomed flameproof casserole. Add chopped onions and garlic, and sauté until vegetables are transparent. Remove vegetables and reserve.

2. Add the meat to the casserole and brown on all sides. Return the onion and garlic, stir in yogurt, spices and flour, and season to taste with salt and freshly ground black pepper. Simmer until tender – about 40 minutes. If desired, thin the sauce with a little light stock before serving.

Veal

36

Veal Chops en Casserole

4-6 thick veal chops
salt and freshly ground black pepper
2 level tablespoons butter
2 tablespoons olive oil

VELOUTÉ SAUCE
2 level tablespoons butter
2 level tablespoons flour
300 ml/½ pint well-flavoured stock

1. Season veal chops generously with salt and freshly ground black pepper.

2. Heat butter and olive oil in a shallow flame-proof earthenware casserole, and simmer veal chops gently on both sides in a moderate oven (160°C, 325°F, Gas Mark 3) until chops are tender.

3. To make Velouté Sauce: melt butter in the top of a double saucepan; stir in flour and cook over water, stirring constantly until smooth. Stir in hot stock and cook, stirring from time to time, until sauce is smooth and thickened.

4. Five minutes before serving, pour sauce over chops. Correct seasoning and serve in the casserole.

Veal with Rosemary

1 rump roast of veal, boned, rolled and tied
salt and freshly ground black pepper
dried thyme
flour
2 level tablespoons butter
2 level tablespoons olive oil
150 ml/¼ pint dry white wine
150 ml/¼ pint water
2 cloves garlic, finely chopped
3 sprigs fresh rosemary
2 Spanish onions, quartered
6 carrots, quartered

1. Season roast generously with salt, freshly ground black pepper and thyme. Dredge with flour. Heat butter and olive oil in a thick-bottomed flameproof casserole, and brown meat on all sides.

2. Add dry white wine, water, finely chopped garlic and rosemary. Cover casserole and cook in a moderate oven (160°C, 325°F, Gas Mark 3) for 1½ hours.

3. Add quartered onions and carrots, and continue to cook until meat and vegetables are tender – 30 to 40 minutes more.

4. Remove roast and vegetables to a heated serving dish. Slice meat and serve with pan juices.

Veal Birds
Illustrated on page 48

12 thin slices veal cutlet
5 level tablespoons butter
1 Spanish onion, finely chopped
100 g/4 oz mushrooms, finely chopped
450 ml/¾ pint well-flavoured stock
1 bay leaf
3-4 celery tops
3-4 sprigs parsley
1 level tablespoon flour
salt and freshly ground black pepper

FORCEMEAT STUFFING
100 g/4 oz fresh breadcrumbs
50 g/2 oz suet, freshly grated
4 level tablespoons finely chopped fresh parsley
½ level teaspoon each dried thyme, marjoram and basil
½ level teaspoon grated lemon rind
2 eggs
salt and freshly ground black pepper
water or dry white wine (optional)

1. To make forcemeat stuffing: mix together breadcrumbs, freshly grated suet, finely chopped fresh parsley, dried herbs, lemon rind and eggs. Season generously with salt and freshly ground black pepper. If mixture seems too dry, add a little water or dry white wine.

2. Beat thin slices of veal with a rolling pin to flatten and tenderise them. Spread forcemeat mixture on each piece of meat, roll up and secure with very fine string.

3. Heat 2 tablespoons butter in a thick-bottomed saucepan and sauté finely chopped onion and mushrooms until onion is transparent.

4. Remove vegetables, add 2 tablespoons butter to pan and cook veal 'birds' over a moderate heat until well browned. Pour in stock and add sautéed mushrooms and onions, bay leaf, celery tops and parsley. Cover pan and simmer gently for 30 to 40 minutes, or until meat is tender.

5. Just before serving, remove strings from veal birds and thicken gravy with a *beurre manié*, made by mashing together 1 tablespoon butter and 1 tablespoon flour. Correct seasoning and serve immediately.

Braised Shoulder of Veal

1 shoulder of veal (about 1.25 kg/2½ lb)
salt and freshly ground black pepper
2–3 level tablespoons butter
2–3 tablespoons olive oil
100 g/4 oz onions
4 carrots
2 sticks celery
3 cloves garlic
2–3 level tablespoons flour
2 bay leaves
450 ml/¾ pint water
450 ml/¾ pint dry white wine
watercress

1. Season veal generously with salt and freshly ground black pepper. Heat butter and olive oil in a large flameproof casserole and brown veal on all sides in fat. Remove veal.

2. Chop onions, carrots, celery and garlic, and brown them in the pan, stirring constantly.

Sprinkle with flour and stir until flour is absorbed by the *mirepoix* of vegetables.

3. Return veal to the pan and add bay leaves, water and dry white wine. Cover the casserole and cook in a moderate oven (160°C, 325°F, Gas Mark 3) for 1½ hours. Turn the meat at least once during cooking time.

4. When veal is tender, strain pan juices into a clean saucepan and reduce the sauce over high heat to half the original quantity. Season the sauce to taste, adding a little more white wine (or cognac) if desired. The flavour of the sauce should be quite pronounced to enhance the rather mild taste of the veal.

5. Carve half the braised veal into rather thick slices. Arrange slices on a heated serving platter with remaining unsliced veal. Spoon some of the sauce over the meat and garnish dish with sprigs of fresh watercress. Serve remaining sauce separately.

Veau à la Ménagère

1.25 kg/2½ lb veal, in 1 piece
4 level tablespoons butter
2 level tablespoons flour
hot water or light stock
1 bay leaf
thyme
salt and freshly ground black pepper
12 mushroom caps
1 (227-g/8-oz) packet frozen peas
12 button onions, blanched
12 small carrots, blanched

1. Melt butter in the bottom of a flameproof casserole. Stir in flour and allow to colour, stirring continuously. Brown veal in this on all sides.

2. Add hot water or light stock and stir constantly until liquid comes to the boil. Add bay leaf, thyme and salt and freshly ground black pepper, to taste. Simmer gently, covered, for 1 hour.

3. Add mushroom caps, peas, and blanched button onions and small carrots. Continue to cook until meat and vegetables are tender.

37

Veal in Soured Cream

**1.5 kg/3 lb lean veal, cut from shoulder or
    leg**
salt and freshly ground black pepper
4 level tablespoons butter
2 tablespoons olive oil
1 level tablespoon flour
300 ml/½ pint soured cream
¼ level teaspoon paprika
2-4 level tablespoons finely chopped onion
225 g/8 oz button mushrooms, quartered
boiled rice to serve

1. Cut veal into 3.5-cm/1½-inch cubes. Season
generously with salt and freshly ground black
pepper, rubbing seasoning well into meat.

2. Heat 2 tablespoons each butter and oil in a
thick-bottomed frying pan, and sauté meat, 4 to 6
pieces at a time, until lightly browned on all sides.

3. Place meat in a flameproof casserole; add flour
to fat remaining in pan and cook, stirring constantly, until smooth. Then add soured cream
and cook, stirring, until well blended. Season to
taste with salt, freshly ground black pepper and
paprika.

4. Melt remaining butter in a separate saucepan
and simmer chopped onion until golden. Add
quartered mushrooms and simmer over a low
heat for 5 minutes.

5. Combine mushroom-onion mixture with
soured cream sauce; add a little hot water if
necessary, and pour over veal. Cover casserole
and bake in a moderate oven (160°C, 325°F, Gas
Mark 3) for 1 hour, or until meat is tender. Serve
with boiled rice.

Veal Fricassée

1.5 kg/3 lb rump or shoulder of veal
lemon juice
butter
2 Spanish onions, chopped
4 large carrots, sliced
2 level tablespoons flour
450 ml/¾ pint dry white wine
well-flavoured veal or chicken stock
salt and freshly ground black pepper
1 bouquet garni (2 sprigs parsley, 2 sprigs
  thyme, 1 bay leaf)
4 leeks, cut in thin strips
12 button mushroom caps
4 egg yolks
400 ml/14 fl oz double cream
1 level tablespoon each finely chopped
  tarragon, chervil and parsley
freshly grated nutmeg

1. Cut veal into 3.5-cm/1½-inch cubes and soak for 12 hours in cold water with a little lemon juice. Change water 2 or 3 times.

2. Sauté blanched veal pieces in butter in a deep flameproof casserole until golden. Add onion and carrots and continue to simmer, stirring from time to time, until onion is transparent. Sprinkle with flour and sauté a few minutes more. Add dry white wine and just enough well-flavoured stock to cover meat. Season with salt and freshly ground black pepper, and bring to the boil. Remove any scum that forms on the surface with a perforated spoon as you would for a *pot-au-feu*. Add *bouquet garni*. Reduce heat, cover casserole and simmer gently over a very low heat or in a cool oven (150°C, 300°F, Gas Mark 2) for 1½ hours, or until tender.

3. Wash leeks thoroughly and cook in a little salted water until tender. Drain and keep warm in a little butter.

4. Simmer mushroom caps in a little butter and lemon juice, and keep warm.

5. Whisk egg yolks with double cream. Pour a little of the hot stock into the cream and egg mixture, whisking to prevent eggs from curdling.

Then add mixture to hot stock in casserole and heat through, being careful not to let mixture come to the boil.

6. Stir mushroom caps, leeks and finely chopped herbs carefully into the fricassée. Season with a little grated nutmeg and keep warm in the oven until ready to serve.

Pot-roasted Veal with Anchovies

1 leg of veal (about 2.75 kg/6 lb)
1 (56-g/2-oz) can anchovy fillets, cut in thin
  strips
2 cloves garlic, cut in thin strips
butter
salt and freshly ground black pepper
4-6 cloves
2 Spanish onions, sliced
2 bay leaves
150 ml/¼ pint dry white wine
150 ml/¼ pint water
4 level tablespoons fine breadcrumbs
1 level tablespoon flour

1. Trim and wipe leg of veal. Make small incisions all over the surface with tip of a sharp knife; stuff incisions with thin anchovy and garlic strips. Rub with 2 tablespoons softened butter, sprinkle with salt and freshly ground black pepper, and insert cloves.

2. Place roast in an ovenproof casserole and surround with sliced onions, bay leaves, dry white wine, water and 2 tablespoons butter. Cover casserole and roast in a moderate oven (160°C, 325°F, Gas Mark 3) for about 3½ hours, basting with pan juices from time to time.

3. Turn roast over, dust with breadcrumbs, dot with 2 tablespoons butter and roast 15 minutes longer, or until crumbs are browned.

4. Transfer veal to a heated serving dish and keep warm. Stir *beurre manié* – made by mashing together 1 tablespoon each flour and butter – into pan juices, and cook, stirring constantly, until sauce is thick. Strain gravy around roast and serve immediately.

40

Osso Buco à l'Orange

4-6 thick slices shin of veal
flour
salt and freshly ground black pepper
4-6 tablespoons olive oil
4 cloves garlic, finely chopped
1 Spanish onion, finely chopped
150 ml/¼ pint boiling chicken or veal stock
150 ml/¼ pint dry white wine
6 level tablespoons tomato purée
6 anchovy fillets, finely chopped
6 level tablespoons finely chopped parsley
grated rind of 1 orange
grated rind of ½ lemon

RISOTTO ALLA MILANESE
½ Spanish onion, finely chopped
4 tablespoons butter
350 g/12 oz rice
hot chicken or veal stock
½ teaspoon powdered saffron
salt and freshly ground black pepper

1. Choose shin of veal with plenty of meat and ask for it to be sawn into pieces 5 cm/2 inches thick. Dredge pieces with flour, season generously with salt and freshly ground black pepper, and simmer in olive oil until lightly browned on all sides.

2. Add 1 clove garlic and 1 Spanish onion, finely chopped. Pour boiling stock, white wine and tomato purée over meat, cover pan and simmer gently for 1½ hours.

3. Add anchovy fillets and the remaining garlic cloves, both finely chopped. Blend thoroughly, heat through and serve sprinkled with finely chopped parsley and grated orange and lemon rind. Serve with *Risotto alla Milanese*.

4. **To cook Risotto alla Milanese:** place finely chopped Spanish onion in a deep saucepan with butter. Cook slowly for 2 to 4 minutes, taking care that the onion does not become brown. Add rice and cook over medium heat, stirring constantly with a wooden spoon. After a minute or so, stir in 250 ml/8 fl oz hot chicken or veal stock in which you have dissolved ½ teaspoon powdered saffron. Continue cooking, adding stock as needed and stirring from time to time, until rice is cooked – 15 to 18 minutes. Correct seasoning. By this time all the stock in the pan should have been absorbed, leaving rice tender but still moist.

Noix de Veau à la Bourgeoise

bacon, cut in thin strips
2 tablespoons cognac
2 level tablespoons finely chopped parsley
dried thyme
salt and freshly ground black pepper
1.25-1.5 kg/2½-3 lb noix de veau (topside of leg), trimmed of fat and tied
pork fat
3-4 onions
3-4 large carrots
6-8 sprigs parsley
1 bouquet chives
300 ml/½ pint beef, veal or chicken stock

SAUCE
2 level tablespoons butter
1 level tablespoon flour
4-6 tablespoons dry white wine
300 ml/½ pint stock
4 tablespoons butter, diced

1. Marinate thin strips of bacon in cognac with finely chopped parsley, and dried thyme, salt and freshly ground black pepper, to taste, for at least 2 hours.

2. Lard the veal with these pieces.

3. Place several thin pieces of pork fat in a casserole (I use an oval Le Creuset casserole for this) and place veal on top. Surround with onions, carrots, parsley and chives, and moisten with well-flavoured stock. Cook over a medium heat until liquid begins to boil. Reduce heat, cover casserole and simmer for 1½ to 2 hours, until veal is tender. Remove veal to a heated serving dish and keep warm.

4. Reduce pan juices over high heat to a quarter of original quantity and glaze veal with several tablespoons of this sauce. Keep warm.

5. To make sauce: melt butter in the top of a double saucepan, add flour and stir until smooth. Add dry white wine, the remaining pan juices and stock, and cook over water, stirring constantly, until smooth. Reduce sauce over a high heat, stirring from time to time. Whisk in diced butter. Serve with the roast.

Tendrons de Veau en Terrine

1.25 kg/2½ lb breast of veal, cut into cutlets
lemon juice
4 level tablespoons butter
2 level tablespoons flour
450 ml/¾ pint well-flavoured Velouté Sauce
**   (see page 90)**
1 bouquet garni (2 sprigs parsley, 2 sprigs
**   thyme, 1 bay leaf)**
4–6 peppercorns
8 button onions, blanched
4 sweetbreads, blanched and sliced
8 button mushroom caps
2 egg yolks
2 level tablespoons finely chopped parsley

1. Soak veal 'cutlets' overnight in water and the juice of 1 lemon.

2. Drain and sauté in butter until they begin to stiffen. Sprinkle with flour and continue to cook, stirring constantly, until veal begins to take on a little colour. Moisten with Velouté Sauce, add *bouquet garni*, peppercorns and blanched button onions, and simmer, covered, for 1 hour.

3. Then add sliced blanched sweetbreads and button mushroom caps, and continue to cook for 45 to 60 minutes longer.

4. Strain, reserving sauce, and place veal, sweetbreads and vegetables in a clean *terrine*.

5. Mix egg yolks with juice of ½ lemon and add a little of the hot sauce to this mixture. Pour egg mixture into rest of hot sauce and cook, stirring constantly, until thick and smooth. Do not allow the sauce to boil, or the yolks will curdle. Pour sauce over veal and sweetbreads, sprinkle with finely chopped parsley and serve.

Pork and Ham

Fillet of Pork with Turnips
Smothered Pork Chops *Serves 4 to 6*
Pork à la Berrichonne

42

Fillet of Pork with Turnips

1 fillet of pork
6 tablespoons water
salt and freshly ground black pepper
18-24 baby turnips
4 level tablespoons butter
fat from pork
2 level tablespoons sugar
150 ml/¼ pint beef stock flavoured with 1-2
   tablespoons tomato purée

1. Ask your butcher to trim and tie a fillet of pork. Put it in a casserole with water, and season to taste with salt and freshly ground black pepper. Cook uncovered in a moderately hot oven (200°C, 400°F, Gas Mark 6) for 20 minutes, or until meat is nicely browned.

2. Blanch turnips in boiling water for 10 minutes, then drain. Sauté turnips in a large thick-bottomed casserole with butter and a little fat from the roast. Sprinkle with sugar and season to taste with salt and freshly ground black pepper. Simmer, shaking pan from time to time, until turnips are glazed.

3. When pork is three-quarters cooked: skim off excess fat, surround with glazed turnips and moisten with tomato-flavoured stock. Cover pan and simmer in a moderate oven (160°C, 325°F, Gas Mark 3) for 20 to 30 minutes or until pork is tender, turning meat from time to time.

Smothered Pork Chops

4-6 loin pork chops
butter
2 level tablespoons olive oil
salt and freshly ground black pepper
dried thyme
4 large potatoes, peeled and thinly sliced
2 large Spanish onions, thinly sliced
450 ml/¾ pint well-flavoured beef stock
4 level tablespoons finely chopped parsley
6 level tablespoons fresh breadcrumbs

1. Sauté pork chops in 2 level tablespoons softened butter and olive oil in a large flameproof casserole

for 5 minutes on one side. Season generously with salt, freshly ground black pepper and dried thyme, and sauté gently for 5 minutes on other side.

2. Spread thinly sliced potatoes over chops. Season with salt and freshly ground black pepper and dried thyme. Spread thinly sliced onions over potatoes and pour over well-flavoured beef stock. Cover casserole and cook in a moderately hot oven (190°C, 375°F, Gas Mark 5) for 35 minutes, or until vegetables and meat are well cooked. Add a little more beef stock or water, during cooking time, if necessary.

3. Remove cover and sprinkle with finely chopped parsley and breadcrumbs. Dribble with melted butter and continue to bake for 10 minutes, or until crumbs are lightly browned.

Pork à la Berrichonne

½ leg of pork, boned and rolled (about
   1.75-2.25 kg/4-5 lb)
600 ml/1 pint dry white wine
salt and freshly ground black pepper
4 carrots, sliced
1 Spanish onion, finely chopped
2 cloves garlic, finely chopped
4 sprigs thyme
6 sage leaves
1 bay leaf
2 level tablespoons butter
300 ml/½ pint stock

1. Marinate pork overnight in a porcelain or glass bowl in dry white wine with salt, freshly ground black pepper, sliced carrots, finely chopped onion and garlic, and herbs.

2. The next day, remove pork from marinade, wipe dry and sauté in butter in a thick-bottomed flameproof casserole until golden on all sides. Pour off butter and moisten with marinade juices. Simmer uncovered in a moderate oven (160°C, 325°F, Gas Mark 3) for 2 hours until the liquid is reduced. Lower the oven heat to cool (140°C, 275°F, Gas Mark 1). Add stock to the casserole, cover and simmer for 45 to 60 minutes, until pork is tender.

Pork Chops in Cider *Serves 4 to 6*
Flemish Pork Casserole *Serves 4*
Ham and Lentil Casserole *Serves 4 to 6*

3. Remove roast and keep warm. Strain juices through a fine sieve, reheat the sauce and serve with the roast.

Pork Chops in Cider

4-6 pork chops
salt and freshly ground black pepper
2 level tablespoons butter
2 tablespoons olive oil
¼ level teaspoon powdered basil
¼ level teaspoon powdered marjoram
¼ level teaspoon powdered thyme
2 Spanish onions, finely chopped
150 ml/¼ pint cider
150 ml/¼ pint water

1. Trim excess fat from pork chops, season generously with salt and freshly ground black pepper, and sauté in butter and olive oil until brown on both sides.

2. Transfer chops to an ovenproof baking dish and sprinkle with basil, marjoram and thyme.

3. Simmer finely chopped onions in remaining fat until transparent. Add to pork chops and moisten with cider and water. Cover the casserole and bake in a moderate oven (180°C, 350°F, Gas Mark 4) for 45 to 60 minutes, until tender. Serve from the casserole.

Flemish Pork Casserole

4 thick pork chops
4 tablespoons butter
4 tart eating apples
6 sprigs rosemary, chopped
salt and freshly ground black pepper
watercress

1. Trim excess fat from chops, season and brown slowly on both sides in 2 tablespoons butter.

2. Peel apples and cut into eighths.

3. Put the half-cooked chops in a shallow ovenproof casserole, sprinkle with rosemary, salt and

freshly ground black pepper, and arrange mounds of apples around them. Sprinkle over remaining butter, melted, and bake in a moderately hot oven (190°C, 375°F, Gas Mark 5) for about 30 minutes, or until pork is thoroughly cooked.

4. Decorate the chops with paper ruffs, garnish with watercress and serve from the casserole.

Ham and Lentil Casserole

225 g/8 oz dried lentils
cooked ham bone (or 225 g/8 oz bacon, in 1 piece)
2 Spanish onions, quartered
2 bay leaves
2 cloves garlic
4 sticks celery, thickly sliced
4 carrots, thickly sliced
salt and freshly ground black pepper
900 ml/1½ pints chicken stock (made with a stock cube)
6 frankfurters
4 level tablespoons finely chopped spring onion tops
4 level tablespoons finely chopped parsley
soured cream to serve

1. Put lentils in a large bowl, cover with cold water, and soak for several hours, or overnight.

2. Drain lentils and put them in a large ovenproof casserole. Add ham shank or bacon piece, quartered onions, bay leaves, garlic and thickly sliced celery and carrots. Season with salt and freshly ground black pepper, to taste. Add chicken stock, cover casserole and cook in a moderate oven (180°C, 350°F, Gas Mark 4) for 1 hour, adding a little more stock if necessary.

3. Add frankfurters, cover casserole and continue to cook for 30 to 45 minutes, until lentils are meltingly tender.

4. To serve: remove ham bone and cut off meat (or remove bacon piece and cut it into slices). Return meat to casserole and correct seasoning. Sprinkle with chopped spring onion tops and parsley and serve immediately with soured cream.

43

44

Cassoulet

675 g/1½ lb dried white haricot beans
450 g/1 lb green bacon, in 1 piece
2 Spanish onions
1 sprig thyme
1 bay leaf
6 cloves garlic
2 tablespoons lard
salt and freshly ground black pepper
675 g/1½ lb boned loin or shoulder of lamb
2 level tablespoons butter
2 tablespoons olive oil
8 saucisses de Toulouse or pork sausages
1 loin of pork (8 thin chops)
8 pieces preserved goose or duck (optional)
8 tomatoes, peeled and seeded
300 ml/½ pint well-flavoured Tomato Sauce (see page 91)
2 level tablespoons pork or goose fat
fresh breadcrumbs

1. To half-cook beans: soak haricot beans overnight. Drain and cook them for 30 minutes in water with bacon, onions, thyme, bay leaf, 3 cloves garlic, lard, and salt and freshly ground black pepper, to taste. Drain, reserving bean stock.

2. To prepare meats: cut lamb into serving pieces and sauté in butter and olive oil in a large flameproof casserole until golden. Remove lamb pieces with a slotted spoon and reserve. Prick the sausages and sauté in fats until golden. Remove and reserve. Then place pork loin in the casserole and sauté over a high heat until golden on all sides. Place casserole in a moderate oven (180°C, 350°F, Gas Mark 4) and roast until well cooked.

3. To assemble dish: place lamb pieces in bottom of a large earthenware casserole and put loin of pork in centre. Add half-cooked beans. Add preserved goose or duck, if desired, and bacon (cut into slices), remaining garlic and tomatoes. Top with more beans, then add sausages and a thin layer of beans (the sausages should not be entirely covered). Pour over the tomato sauce, add 300–600 ml/½–1 pint bean stock and 2 tablespoons pork or goose fat. Sprinkle generously with breadcrumbs and cook in a cool oven (150°C, 300°F, Gas Mark 2) for 2½ hours. Cover dish with aluminium foil after the first hour of cooking so that it does not form too thick a crust.

Choucroute Garnie au Champagne
Illustrated opposite

fat salt pork, thinly sliced
2 Spanish onions, sliced
4 cloves garlic, coarsely chopped
1.75 kg/4 lb sauerkraut, well washed
450 g/1 lb salt pork, in 1 piece
freshly ground black pepper
4–6 juniper berries
champagne or white wine
1 boned loin of pork
1 large Lorraine sausage, or 1 Cotechino sausage and 4–8 other sausages (Bratwurst, Knockwurst, frankfurters, saucisses de Toulouse)
boiled potatoes to serve

1. Line a deep earthenware casserole or stockpot with thinly sliced fat salt pork. Add half the sliced onions and chopped garlic. Place a thick layer of well-washed and drained sauerkraut on top with a large piece of salt pork. Grind plenty of black pepper over it, sprinkle with juniper berries, and add remaining onions and garlic. Cover with remaining sauerkraut and add just enough champagne (or white wine) to cover the sauerkraut. Cover and cook in a cool oven (150°C, 300°F, Gas Mark 2) for 4 to 6 hours.

2. A loin of pork, fresh or smoked, is excellent with *choucroute*. Add it to the *choucroute* about 2½ hours before serving.

3. Half an hour later add a large Lorraine sausage (or a Cotechino sausage, and a selection of small sausages as available).

4. To serve: heap the *choucroute* in the middle of a platter and arrange slices of meat and sausages around it. For those with a taste for the spectacular – place an unopened half-bottle of champagne, with only the wires removed, in the centre of the hot sauerkraut just before bringing it to the table. Then watch the warmed champagne gush out over the sauerkraut. Serve with boiled potatoes.

Choucroute Garnie au Champagne (see page 44)

Carne Assada (Portuguese Pot Roast) (see page 22)

Veal Birds (see page 36)

Stufatino di Manzo (see page 20)

Petit Salé aux Choux *Serves 4 to 6*
Potée Bourguignonne *Serves 6*
Ham and Egg Luncheon Casserole *Serves 4 to 6*

Petit Salé aux Choux

675 g/1½ lb pickled or salted pork
1 bouquet garni (2 sprigs parsley, 2 sprigs
    thyme, 2 bay leaves)
1 Spanish onion, stuck with 2 cloves
peppercorns
1 medium-sized cabbage
boiled potatoes (optional)

1. Wash pickled or salted pork and soak, covered, for 24 hours in cold water, changing water several times.

2. Put fresh water in a large flameproof casserole, add meat and bring gently to the boil. Skim well and add *bouquet garni*, onion stuck with cloves, and peppercorns.

3. Clean cabbage and cut into wedges, and add it to the boiling liquid. Reduce heat and simmer meat and vegetables for about 2 hours.

4. Remove cabbage and drain well. Place it in a shallow serving bowl, place meat on top and surround, if desired, with boiled potatoes. The pot liquor will serve to make lentil or pea soup.

Potée Bourguignonne

675 g/1½ lb pickled or salted pork
6 sausages
100 g/4 oz bacon, in 1 piece
225 g/8 oz turnips
225 g/8 oz carrots
1 Spanish onion
1 bouquet garni (2 sprigs parsley, 2 sprigs
    thyme, 1 bay leaf, 1 stick celery)
peppercorns
1 small cabbage
450 g/1 lb small potatoes, peeled

1. Soak meat, covered, in cold water for 24 hours, changing water several times.

2. Put the salt pork, sausages and bacon in a flameproof casserole with cold water. Bring gently to the boil. Skim and simmer gently for 30 minutes, skimming from time to time.

3. Peel turnips, carrots and Spanish onion. Add vegetables to *pot-au-feu* with *bouquet garni* and peppercorns. Skim. Reduce heat and simmer for 1 hour.

4. Cut cabbage into 6 wedges. Cook in gently simmering salted water until just tender. Drain. Add peeled potatoes to casserole and continue to cook for 40 minutes longer. Just before serving, put cabbage wedges in casserole and heat through.

5. To serve potée: remove vegetables from *bouillon* with a slotted spoon. Place cabbage in a shallow serving bowl, place the salt pork on it and surround with sausages, bacon cut into thin slices, and vegetables. Moisten with a little *bouillon*. The remaining *bouillon* will serve as the base for an excellent soup.

Ham and Egg Luncheon Casserole

6 eggs
2–3 Spanish onions
2 level tablespoons butter
2 tablespoons olive oil
225 g/8 oz ham, in 1 piece, cut into dice
450 ml/¾ pint light Béchamel Sauce (see
    page 91)
salt and freshly ground black pepper
2 level tablespoons finely chopped parsley

1. Hard-boil the eggs for 15 minutes in boiling water. Remove shells and slice.

2. Slice onions and sauté in butter and olive oil in a shallow flameproof casserole until they are soft and golden; do not let them brown.

3. Add diced ham and continue to cook, stirring, until onions just start to turn colour. Add hot Béchamel Sauce to onion and ham mixture and stir well. Fold in the egg slices and add salt and freshly ground black pepper, to taste. Heat through, sprinkle with finely chopped parsley and serve immediately.

49

Vegetable

Braised Celery

2 heads celery
½ Spanish onion, thinly sliced
2 small carrots, thinly sliced
butter
150 ml/¼ pint chicken stock
salt and freshly ground black pepper
1 level tablespoon flour
finely chopped parsley

1. Clean celery, cut each head in half lengthwise and trim off tops. Blanch celery in boiling water for 10 minutes.

2. Drain carefully and put in a flameproof casserole with thinly sliced onion, carrots, 2 level tablespoons butter and chicken stock. Season to taste with salt and freshly ground black pepper. Cover casserole and cook gently until tender (30 to 40 minutes), adding a little more stock, if necessary.

3. Five minutes before you remove vegetables from heat, mix 1 tablespoon each butter and flour to a smooth paste and stir into pan juices to thicken sauce. Just before serving sprinkle with finely chopped parsley.

French Potato and Cheese Casserole

675 g-1 kg/1½-2 lb new potatoes
butter
150 ml/¼ pint well-flavoured beef stock
6 level tablespoons freshly grated Gruyère
cheese
2 level tablespoons freshly grated Parmesan
cheese
salt and freshly ground black pepper

1. Butter an ovenproof shallow casserole.

2. Peel and slice potatoes thinly and soak in cold water for a few minutes. Drain and dry thoroughly with a clean tea towel. Place a layer of sliced potatoes on bottom of casserole in overlapping rows. Pour over a quarter of the stock, sprinkle with 2 tablespoons grated cheese (mixed Gruyère and Parmesan), dot with butter and season to taste with salt and freshly ground black pepper (not too much salt). Continue this process until casserole is full, finishing with a layer of grated cheese. Dot with butter and cook in a moderate oven (180°C, 350°F, Gas Mark 4) for about 1 hour, or until potatoes are cooked through. If top becomes too brown, cover with aluminium foil. Serve very hot.

Braised Chicory

8 heads chicory
butter
½ Spanish onion, thinly sliced
2 small carrots, thinly sliced
150 ml/¼ pint chicken stock
salt and freshly ground black pepper
juice of ½ lemon or orange
1 level tablespoon butter
½ level tablespoon flour

1. Trim root ends of chicory and wash well in cold water. Drain.

2. Heat 4 tablespoons butter in a shallow flame-proof casserole. Add raw chicory, thinly sliced onion, carrots and chicken stock. Season to taste with salt and freshly ground black pepper. Cover vegetables with buttered paper. Cover casserole and simmer over a very low heat or in a moderate oven (180°C, 350°F, Gas Mark 4) for 40 minutes, or until tender, adding a little more stock, if necessary.

3. Turn vegetables from time to time and, 20 minutes after putting casserole in the oven, sprinkle vegetables with the juice of ½ lemon or orange.

4. Five minutes before you remove vegetables from heat, mix 1 tablespoon each butter and flour to a smooth paste and stir into pan juices to thicken sauce.

Saffron Cabbage and Ham Casserole

1 small white cabbage
1 small green cabbage
600 ml/1 pint brown stock
225 g/8 oz cooked ham, cut into slivers
1 Spanish onion, thinly sliced
butter
½ level teaspoon saffron
salt and freshly ground black pepper
¼ level teaspoon cayenne

1. Cut cabbages into eighths and soak in salted water for 30 minutes.

2. Drain well and then arrange in a large flame-proof casserole. Pour over stock, cover casserole and simmer in stock for 10 to 15 minutes, until cabbage is just about half done.

3. Sauté ham slivers and thinly sliced onion in a little butter for a few minutes, until onion is soft.

4. Mix saffron with a little hot water and add it to the cabbage together with sautéed ham and onion. Season with salt, freshly ground black pepper and cayenne. Mix thoroughly and simmer until cabbage is tender and not mushy. If it gets too dry while cooking, add a little more stock.

Scalloped Cabbage Casserole

1 cabbage
salt
4 level tablespoons butter
300 ml/½ pint Béchamel Sauce (see page 91)
freshly ground black pepper
4-6 level tablespoons freshly grated
   Parmesan cheese
150 ml/¼ pint double cream
¼ chicken stock cube
freshly grated nutmeg

1. Shred cabbage and soak in salted cold water for 30 minutes. Drain well. Melt butter in a flame-proof casserole, add shredded cabbage and simmer, covered, until cabbage is just tender but not browned.

2. Remove half the simmered cabbage. Pour over cabbage remaining in the casserole half the quantity of Béchamel Sauce. Sprinkle with freshly ground black pepper and half the grated Parmesan.

3. Add remaining cabbage, pour remaining sauce over the top and add more freshly ground black pepper and remainder of Parmesan.

4. Simmer double cream with ¼ chicken stock cube and then pour over cabbage. Sprinkle with a little freshly grated nutmeg. Place casserole in a moderate oven (180°C, 350°F, Gas Mark 4) and cook until the casserole bubbles and the top is golden brown – about 30 minutes.

52

Cabbage Casserole

1 green cabbage (about 1 kg/2 lb)
salt
1 level tablespoon cornflour
450 ml/¾ pint milk
coarsely grated Gruyère cheese
butter
freshly ground black pepper
freshly grated nutmeg

1. Remove and discard discoloured outer leaves from green cabbage. Wash, core and shred cabbage, and soak in cold salted water for 30 minutes. Drain and cook, covered, in a small amount of boiling salted water until just tender. Drain.

2. Mix cornflour with a little hot milk. Bring remaining milk to the boil in the top of a double saucepan, stir in cornflour mixture and cook over boiling water until mixture thickens. Add 6 level tablespoons grated Gruyère, 4 level tablespoons butter, and salt, freshly ground black pepper and nutmeg, to taste. Stir into cabbage and mix well.

3. Turn the mixture into a well-buttered shallow casserole; sprinkle with 2 level tablespoons grated Gruyère, dot with butter and brown lightly in the oven.

Steamed Stuffed Cabbage

1 Savoy cabbage
butter
Italian Tomato Sauce (see page 91)

STUFFING
1 Spanish onion, chopped
butter
225 g/8 oz button mushrooms, chopped
450 g/1 lb cooked ham, pork or veal,
  'finely chopped
8 level tablespoons cooked rice
salt and freshly ground black pepper
freshly grated nutmeg
little chicken stock

1. To make stuffing: sauté chopped onion in 4 tablespoons butter until transparent. Add mush-

rooms and simmer, stirring constantly, until soft. In another pan, sauté ham in 2 tablespoons butter until golden. Combine ham with vegetables and rice, and season generously with salt, freshly ground black pepper and nutmeg. Moisten with chicken stock.

2. Wash, trim and core cabbage. Place it in a large saucepan, cover with water and bring to the boil. Drain well.

3. Cut out centre of cabbage in a circle with a diameter of about 6 cm/2½ inches, and scoop out to form a cup. Beginning with the outer leaves, separate leaves one by one and fill each leaf with 1 to 2 tablespoons stuffing. Spoon remaining stuffing into cavity.

4. Place cabbage in a well-buttered ovenproof dish, cover loosely with foil and steam over boiling water in a covered pan until tender. Serve with Italian Tomato Sauce.

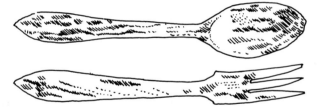

Braised Stuffed Lettuce Leaves

2 lettuces
2 level tablespoons butter
100 g/4 oz raw rice
600 ml/1 pint hot beef stock
1 Spanish onion, finely chopped
6-8 button mushrooms, finely chopped
2 tablespoons olive oil
100 g/4 oz ham, finely chopped
salt and freshly ground black pepper
2 level tablespoons tomato purée
2 level tablespoons finely chopped parsley

1. Separate lettuce leaves and wash well. Drain. Pour over boiling water to soften leaves. Drain.

2. Melt butter in a thick-bottomed frying pan. Add the rice and sauté until golden. Add half the hot beef stock to cover rice (adding a little water, if necessary), and cook, stirring constantly, until mixture comes to the boil. Reduce heat, cover the pan and cook slowly for about 15 minutes, adding a little more beef stock if necessary.

3. Sauté the chopped onion and mushrooms in oil in another frying pan and add to rice mixture. Mix in the finely chopped ham. Season generously with salt and freshly ground black pepper.

4. Place equal quantities of the rice and ham mixture on each lettuce leaf and roll them up, tucking ends in to form a neat 'package'. Arrange lettuce packets in a shallow ovenproof casserole.

5. Blend tomato purée with remaining hot beef stock. Pour over the lettuce packages, cover casserole and cook in a moderately hot oven (190°C, 375°F, Gas Mark 5) for 30 minutes, or until done, basting frequently. Sprinkle with finely chopped parsley and serve from the casserole.

Courgette Casserole

**1 kg/2 lb courgettes, sliced
salt
1 Spanish onion, finely chopped
butter
2 eggs
8 level tablespoons soured cream
8 level tablespoons freshly grated Gruyère
  cheese
freshly ground black pepper
2 level tablespoons dried breadcrumbs**

1. Simmer courgettes in a little salted water in a covered saucepan until tender but still crisp – about 5 minutes. Drain and whisk in an electric blender.

2. Sauté onion in butter until transparent. Add to courgette mixture with eggs, soured cream and 3 tablespoons grated cheese, and blend again. Season generously with salt and freshly ground black pepper.

3. Butter a shallow ovenproof casserole, line it with 3 tablespoons grated cheese and pour in the courgette mixture.

4. Mix breadcrumbs with remaining cheese and sprinkle over the top. Bake in a moderate oven (160°C, 325°F, Gas Mark 3) for 30 to 40 minutes, until set.

Tunisian Pepper and Tomato Casserole

**2 Spanish onions
olive oil
6 ripe tomatoes, sliced
3 red or green peppers, diced
1 (100-g/3¼-oz) can tomato purée
1-2 cloves garlic
salt and freshly ground black pepper
⅛-¼ level teaspoon each cayenne and paprika
4 eggs
powdered cumin**

1. Slice onions thickly and sauté in 6 tablespoons olive oil until golden. Add sliced tomatoes, diced peppers, tomato purée and garlic, and simmer vegetables until soft and cooked through.

2. Add 4 tablespoons olive oil, season to taste with salt, freshly ground black pepper, cayenne and paprika, and simmer for 5 minutes more.

3. To serve: spoon softened vegetables into individual casseroles or ovenproof serving dishes. Break 1 egg into each dish and bake in a moderately hot oven (200°C, 400°F, Gas Mark 6) until eggs are just set – about 10 minutes. Sprinkle with a little powdered cumin.

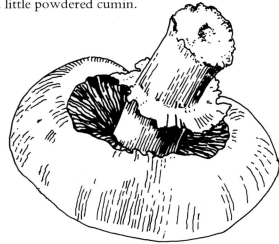

54

French Aubergine Casserole

1 kg/2 lb aubergines
2 Spanish onions, finely chopped
4 cloves garlic, finely chopped
600–900 ml/1–1½ pints chicken stock
salt and freshly ground black pepper
1 bay leaf
100 g/4 oz finely grated Gruyère cheese
4–6 eggs (1 per person)
garlic croûtons

1. Cut the aubergines (unpeeled) into small cubes. Combine with finely chopped onions and garlic in an ovenproof casserole. Add chicken stock, to cover. Season with salt and freshly ground black pepper, to taste, and add bay leaf. Cook in a moderately hot oven (190°C, 375°F, Gas Mark 5) for 20 minutes, stirring once during cooking time. When vegetables are tender, sprinkle with grated Gruyère and cook for 5 minutes more.

2. Just before serving, break 1 egg per person into a small saucer, slide gently into the casserole and continue to cook until egg whites are firm, about 5 minutes.

3. Serve hot with lightly flavoured garlic *croûtons*.

Aubergine and Minced Beef Casserole

1 large onion, coarsely chopped
butter
675 g/1½ lb minced lean beef
150 ml/¼ pint tomato purée
450 ml/¾ pint water
1 level teaspoon salt
¼ level teaspoon freshly ground black pepper
4 medium-sized aubergines, sliced

1. Sauté chopped onion in 4 tablespoons butter until golden. Add the meat and cook, stirring continuously, until it is browned.

2. Combine the tomato purée with the water, add salt and freshly ground black pepper, and pour sauce over meat. Bring to the boil and simmer for 5 minutes. Remove mixture.

3. Sauté aubergine slices in 8 tablespoons butter and place a layer of aubergine in the bottom of a well-buttered casserole.

4. Using a slotted spoon, add a layer of drained beef, another layer of aubergine, then beef, and so on, until all the beef and aubergines have been used up. Pour over the remaining sauce and bake, uncovered, in a moderate oven (180°C, 350°F, Gas Mark 4) until aubergines are tender. Serve hot.

Aubergine and Minced Lamb Casserole
Illustrated on page 28

1 Spanish onion, finely chopped
2 cloves garlic, finely chopped
olive oil
675 g/1½ lb cooked lamb, minced
225 g/8 oz mushrooms, chopped
6 tomatoes, peeled, seeded and chopped
4 level tablespoons finely chopped parsley
salt and freshly ground black pepper
1–2 level tablespoons tomato purée
6 tablespoons rich beef or veal stock
4–6 aubergines, unpeeled
flour
4–6 tablespoons grated Parmesan cheese
2 eggs
1 (142-ml/5-fl oz) carton yogurt

1. Sauté onion and garlic in 4 tablespoons olive oil until transparent. Add lamb and continue cooking, stirring from time to time, until brown. Add chopped mushrooms, tomatoes, parsley, and salt and freshly ground black pepper, to taste, and cook until onion is tender.

2. Dilute tomato purée in stock. Add to meat and vegetable mixture and simmer for 10 minutes.

3. Slice aubergines, unpeeled, in thin slices. Dust with flour and fry on both sides in hot olive oil; drain on absorbent paper. Line a baking dish with slices of aubergine. Spread a layer of stuffing mixture on them, sprinkle lightly with grated Parmesan cheese and cover with a layer of aubergines. Continue this process until baking dish is full, ending with a layer of aubergines.

4. Beat eggs and blend in 2 level tablespoons flour. Add yogurt and whisk to a creamy sauce. Pour this sauce over meat and vegetable mixture. Sprinkle with grated Parmesan cheese and bake in a moderately hot oven (190°C, 375°F, Gas Mark 5) until the top has browned nicely. Serve hot. It is also very good cold and can be reheated successfully.

Ratatouille

8 tablespoons olive oil
2 Spanish onions, sliced
2 cloves garlic, finely chopped
2 green peppers, sliced
2 small aubergines, sliced
4 courgettes, sliced
8 ripe tomatoes, peeled, seeded and chopped
salt and freshly ground black pepper
4 level tablespoons chopped parsley
$\frac{1}{4}$ level teaspoon dried marjoram
$\frac{1}{4}$ level teaspoon dried basil

1. Heat olive oil in a large thick-bottomed flame-proof casserole. Add sliced onions and garlic and sauté until vegetables soften.

2. Add sliced green peppers and aubergines and continue to cook, stirring from time to time. Ten minutes later, stir in sliced courgettes and peeled, seeded and chopped tomatoes. Reduce heat, cover casserole and simmer vegetables gently for 30 minutes.

3. Season to taste with salt and freshly ground black pepper, add chopped parsley, marjoram and basil and cook, uncovered, for about 10 to 15 minutes more. Serve hot from the casserole.

56

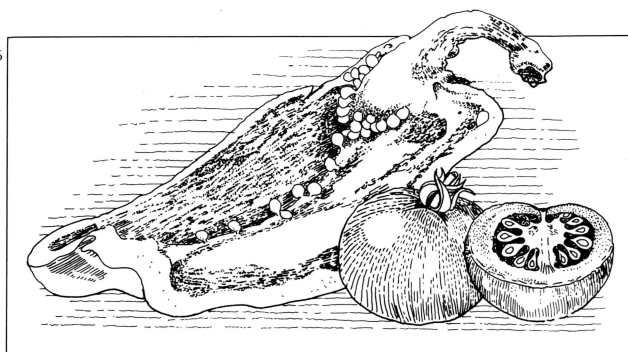

Baked Corn and Courgette Casserole

I Spanish onion, finely chopped
I clove garlic, finely chopped
4 level tablespoons butter, melted
I green pepper, diced
450 g/I lb courgettes, thinly sliced
2 (312-g/II-oz) cans sweet corn niblets
dried oregano and marjoram
salt and freshly ground black pepper
300 ml/½ pint Italian Tomato Sauce (see page 91)

I. Sauté finely chopped onion and garlic in butter in a flameproof casserole until vegetables are transparent. Add diced green pepper and continue to sauté, stirring constantly, until vegetables just begin to change colour. Then add finely sliced courgettes and continue to sauté, stirring continuously, until courgettes begin to soften.

2. Drain corn niblets and add to casserole with dried oregano, or marjoram, and salt and freshly ground black pepper, to taste.

3. Pour over Italian Tomato Sauce and cook, uncovered, in a moderate oven (180°C, 350°F, Gas Mark 4) for about 45 minutes.

Peas and Pasta Luncheon Casserole

2 (227-g/8-oz) packets frozen peas
225 g/8 oz small shell pasta
salt
4 level tablespoons butter
½ Spanish onion, finely chopped
I clove garlic, finely chopped
100 g/4 oz cooked ham, cut into pea-sized dice
2 level tablespoons finely chopped parsley
I chicken stock cube
freshly ground black pepper
freshly grated Gruyère cheese

I. Defrost peas.

2. Cook pasta shells in salted boiling water until just tender. Drain.

3. Melt butter in a large shallow flameproof casserole. Add finely chopped onion and garlic and simmer gently until vegetables are soft. Add diced cooked ham, pasta shells and finely chopped parsley and cook over a low heat, stirring, for several minutes.

4. In the meantime dissolve chicken stock cube in 150 ml/¼ pint hot water and add to casserole with defrosted peas. Season with salt and freshly ground black pepper. Cover casserole and continue to cook for 10 to 15 minutes, until peas are tender.

5. Serve from casserole, with freshly grated Gruyère cheese.

Creole Rice Casserole

225 g/8 oz rice
butter
olive oil
600 ml/1 pint chicken stock
salt and freshly ground black pepper
1 green pepper, diced
1 Spanish onion, chopped
1 (793-g/1 lb 12-oz) can Italian peeled
    tomatoes
4 level tablespoons finely chopped parsley
2 bay leaves, crumbled
4–6 tomatoes, sliced
½ level teaspoon dried oregano
6 level tablespoons freshly grated Gruyère
    cheese
4 level tablespoons freshly grated Parmesan
    cheese

1. Sauté rice in 2 tablespoons each butter and olive oil until rice becomes translucent. Add chicken stock and simmer until rice is just tender. Add more butter, and salt and freshly ground black pepper, to taste.

2. Sauté diced green pepper and chopped onion in 2 tablespoons each butter and olive oil in a large shallow flameproof casserole until vegetables are soft.

3. Chop canned tomatoes coarsely and add, with juices, to casserole. Then stir in chopped parsley, bay leaves and salt and freshly ground black pepper, to taste. Simmer for 3 minutes.

4. Add hot butter-cooked rice to casserole, mix well and top with a layer of overlapping tomato slices. Sprinkle with oregano and freshly grated Gruyère and Parmesan cheese and cook in a moderate oven (180°C, 350°F, Gas Mark 4) for 25 to 30 minutes until cheese has melted and is bubbling brown.

Boston Baked Beans

Illustrated on page 27

675 g/1½ lb haricot beans
450 g/1 lb salt pork or fat bacon
2 onions, finely chopped
2 level teaspoons dry mustard
salt and freshly ground black pepper
4 level tablespoons dark treacle
4 tablespoons Demerara sugar
600 ml/1 pint boiling water from beans
4 level tablespoons tomato ketchup
2 level tablespoons bacon fat
sautéed onion rings, cooked sausages and
    frankfurters (optional)

1. Soak the beans overnight in cold water.

2. Drain, cover again with fresh water, and allow to simmer on a low heat for about 1 hour, or until the skins of the beans burst when blown upon. Drain again, saving about 600 ml/1 pint of the liquid.

3. Scald the salt pork quickly; drain pork and cut slashes in the rind with a sharp knife.

4. Cut pork in 2 pieces; place 1 piece in bottom of a large casserole, add beans and bury remainder of pork in the beans so that the rind just shows.

5. Mix finely chopped onions, mustard, salt, freshly ground black pepper, treacle and sugar with reserved bean water, and bring to the boil. Pour this mixture over the beans, to cover. If necessary, add more boiling water. Place lid on casserole and bake in a cool to moderate oven (150–160°C, 300–325°F, Gas Mark 2–3) for 6 hours. From time to time add more boiling water, so that beans are kept covered and moist.

6. **One hour before serving:** stir 2 to 4 tablespoons tomato ketchup into the beans, drip the hot melted bacon fat over them and cook for 1 hour in a moderate oven, uncovered, to colour beans and brown pork. If desired, add sautéed onion rings, cooked sausages and frankfurters just before serving.

58

Mexican Beans

Illustrated on page 27

450 g/1 lb red kidney beans
1 Spanish onion, finely chopped
2 cloves garlic, finely chopped
salt
2 level tablespoons butter
1 level tablespoon flour
½ level teaspoon cumin powder
2 level tablespoons Mexican chili powder*
1 bouquet garni (2 sprigs parsley, 2 sprigs
   thyme, 1 stick celery, 1 bay leaf)
300 ml/½ pint beef stock
freshly ground black pepper

* Spice Islands brand or Twin Trees or McCormicks – not powdered chillies.

1. Place kidney beans in a large saucepan. Fill pan with water and bring gently to the boil. Remove saucepan from heat and let beans soak in hot water for 1 hour.

2. Drain, and simmer with finely chopped onion and garlic in salted water in a large casserole. After about 1 hour of cooking, taste them. If they are cooked, drain; if not, continue to simmer until they are tender, but do not let them burst. Drain.

3. Mix butter, flour, cumin powder and Mexican chili powder (a combination of powdered chillies, cumin, salt, flour and garlic) to a smooth paste.

4. Combine cooked beans and chili paste in a saucepan and add *bouquet garni*, beef stock, and salt and freshly ground black pepper, to taste. Simmer, stirring gently from time to time, for about 45 minutes, until sauce is smooth and rich.

5. Remove *bouquet garni*. Serve immediately.

Red Beans and Bacon

450 g/1 lb red kidney beans
2 Spanish onions, chopped
1 bouquet garni (2 sprigs parsley, 2 sprigs
   thyme, 1 stick celery, 1 bay leaf)
1 strip orange peel
450 g/1 lb bacon, in 1 piece
150–300 ml/¼–½ pint red wine
4-6 tablespoons olive oil
salt and freshly ground black pepper

1. Place kidney beans in a large saucepan. Fill pan with water and bring gently to the boil. Remove pan from heat and let beans soak for 1 hour.

2. Drain; simmer beans with chopped onions, *bouquet garni*, orange peel and bacon in water to cover in a large casserole until beans are almost cooked through – 45 to 60 minutes. Beans should remain fairly firm, otherwise they will break in subsequent cooking. Add a little more water from time to time, if necessary. Remove bacon and keep warm. Drain beans, reserving liquid.

3. Combine drained beans with about 150 ml/¼ pint of the reserved bean liquor in a clean casserole. Add red wine, olive oil and salt and freshly ground black pepper, to taste, and simmer gently, stirring beans from time to time, for about 10 minutes, or until beans have absorbed flavour. Remove *bouquet garni*.

4. Slice bacon; add to the casserole and serve immediately.

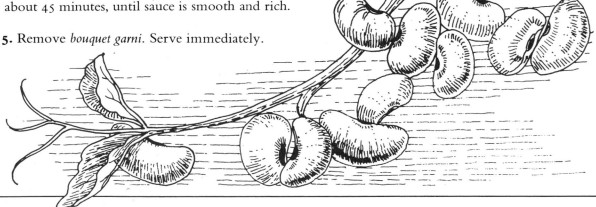

Poultry

Chicken en Cocotte

Illustrated on page 66

1 tender chicken (about 1.5 kg/3½ lb)
salt and freshly ground black pepper
225 g/8 oz fat bacon, in 1 piece
2 level tablespoons butter
2 tablespoons olive oil
1 Spanish onion, finely chopped
1 clove garlic, finely chopped
1 bouquet garni (2 sprigs parsley, 2 sprigs
  thyme, 1 bay leaf)
300 ml/½ pint dry white wine

1. Cut chicken into serving pieces and season to taste with salt and freshly ground black pepper.

2. Cut bacon into 'fingers', about 5 mm/¼ inch thick.

3. Heat butter and oil in an iron *cocotte* or a heavy casserole and sauté bacon 'fingers' until golden.

4. Remove bacon and reserve. Add finely chopped onion and garlic and cook over a medium heat, stirring constantly, until soft. Remove with a slotted spoon. Add chicken pieces to casserole and brown them on all sides.

5. Return bacon, onion and garlic to the pan, then add *bouquet garni* and dry white wine. Cover the casserole and let the chicken simmer over a very low heat until it is tender. Add a little chicken stock (made with a cube), during the cooking, if the sauce reduces too quickly.

Braised Chicken with Tomatoes

1 tender chicken (about 1.5 kg/3½ lb)
2 tablespoons olive oil
4 level tablespoons butter
450 g/1 lb tomatoes, peeled, seeded and
  coarsely chopped
1 clove garlic, finely chopped
6 level tablespoons finely chopped onion
salt and freshly ground black pepper
300 ml/½ pint well-flavoured chicken stock
4-6 tablespoons dry sherry
2 level tablespoons finely chopped parsley

1. Prepare and truss chicken.

2. Melt olive oil and 2 level tablespoons butter in a thick-bottomed flameproof casserole, and brown chicken in it on all sides.

3. Melt remaining butter in a frying pan, and sauté tomatoes, garlic and onion until onion is soft.

4. Add vegetables to the browned chicken, season with salt and freshly ground black pepper, and pour in the stock. Cover casserole, place in a moderate oven (160°C, 325°F, Gas Mark 3) for 1½ to 2 hours until chicken is tender. If necessary, a little more stock may be added during the cooking.

5. To serve: place chicken on a hot serving dish and remove trussing thread or string. Skim fat from tomatoes, add dry sherry and correct seasoning. Sprinkle with finely chopped parsley and pour sauce around the chicken.

Chicken en Casserole

1 chicken (about 1.5 kg/3½ lb)
6 small white onions
4 carrots, diced
2 turnips, diced
2 sticks celery, sliced
2 bay leaves
300 ml/½ pint well-flavoured chicken stock
salt and freshly ground black pepper

1. Prepare and truss chicken. Put it in an oven-proof casserole with peeled white onions, diced carrot and turnip, sliced celery and bay leaves.

2. Heat chicken stock and add to casserole. Cover and cook in a moderate oven (160°C, 325°F, Gas Mark 3) for 1½ to 2 hours, until the chicken is quite tender, basting occasionally with the stock. Season with salt and freshly ground black pepper.

3. Cut chicken into serving pieces. Serve in casserole.

Saffron Chicken Casserole

1 chicken (about 1.5 kg/3½ lb)
100 g/4 oz butter
1 Spanish onion, finely chopped
1 chicken stock cube
¼–½ level teaspoon saffron
salt and freshly ground black pepper
hot water
300 ml/½ pint cream
4 egg yolks

1. Cut chicken into 8 serving pieces. Melt butter in a large flameproof casserole, and sauté chicken pieces gently on all sides without letting them colour.

2. Add finely chopped onion, crumbled chicken stock cube, saffron, and salt and freshly ground black pepper, to taste. Cover with hot water and simmer gently for 50 to 60 minutes, until tender.

3. Just before serving, whisk cream and egg yolks together in a large bowl. Remove chicken pieces with a slotted spoon. Strain a little hot chicken stock into cream and egg mixture and whisk. Strain remainder of stock into bowl, pressing all juices through sieve.

4. Clean casserole, return chicken pieces to it and pour creamy mixture over chicken. Heat through for 5 minutes, stirring continuously, being careful that sauce never comes to the boil or the sauce will curdle. Correct seasoning and serve immediately.

Summer Saffron Chicken

1 tender chicken (about 1.5 kg/3½ lb)
butter
12 small onions
1 level tablespoon flour
½ level teaspoon saffron
salt and freshly ground black pepper
1 bouquet garni (2 sprigs parsley, 2 sprigs thyme, 1 bay leaf)
24 button mushrooms
juice of 2 lemons
2 egg yolks
300 ml/½ pint double cream

1. Cut chicken into 8 serving pieces and sauté in 4 to 6 tablespoons butter with onions in a large flameproof casserole until chicken pieces just begin to turn colour. Sprinkle chicken pieces and onions with flour and add just enough water to cover chicken. Season with saffron, and salt and freshly ground black pepper, to taste. Add *bouquet garni,* cover casserole and cook for about 1½ hours, or until chicken is tender.

2. Remove chicken and onions to a deep serving dish or clean casserole. Strain stock into a clean saucepan and reserve.

3. Sauté button mushrooms in 2 tablespoons butter and juice of 1 lemon until tender and add to chicken and onions. Chill.

4. Whisk egg yolks, juice of 1 lemon and 150 ml/ ¼ pint double cream in a bowl. Bring stock to the boil, and add, whisking vigorously, a ladle of boiling stock to the cream and egg mixture. Pour mixture into the hot stock, bring gently to the boil, whisking well, until sauce is thick and creamy. Strain sauce through a fine sieve into a clean bowl and allow to cool. Chill.

5. When ready to serve, whisk remaining cream into cold saffron sauce, correct seasoning and spoon over chicken and vegetables. Toss well.

Poulet aux Concombres

4 medium-sized carrots
1 Spanish onion
1 tender chicken (about 1.5 kg/3½ lb),
    with giblets
melted butter
¼ level teaspoon powdered thyme
1 bay leaf, crumbled
salt
2 large firm tomatoes, peeled, seeded and
    coarsely chopped
1 cucumber
freshly ground black pepper
150 ml/¼ pint double cream
paprika

1. Slice carrots and onion thinly, chop giblets; place in the bottom of a well-buttered flameproof casserole. Heat gently for 5 minutes.

2. Place chicken, brushed with 100 g/4 oz melted butter, on top of this bed of vegetables and cook in a moderate oven (180°C, 350°F, Gas Mark 4) for 45 minutes, turning the chicken several times, as it cooks, basting well each time.

3. Fifteen minutes after putting in the chicken, add powdered thyme and bay leaf, a sprinkle of salt and coarsely chopped tomatoes.

4. Peel cucumber, cut into halves lengthwise, and remove seeds with a pointed teaspoon. Cut into 5-cm/2-inch segments and round off the edges to make prettier shapes. Blanch cucumber segments in boiling salted water for 3 minutes. Remove and drain. Season with salt and freshly ground black pepper and simmer gently in 100 g/4 oz butter and 150 ml/¼ pint double cream in a small pan with a tight-fitting lid. Season with salt and paprika, to taste.

5. When the chicken is tender, transfer it, with vegetables, to a warm serving dish. Pour remaining sauce from cucumbers into the casserole in which the chicken has been cooked, bring to the boil and simmer for 2 minutes. Check seasoning and strain over chicken. Arrange the cucumber segments around chicken and serve immediately.

Poulet aux Poivrons

1 roasting chicken (about 1.5 kg/3½ lb when
    cleaned)
2 level tablespoons butter
2 tablespoons olive oil
½ level teaspoon paprika
salt and freshly ground black pepper
cayenne
2 Spanish onions, finely chopped
4 cloves garlic, finely chopped
1 kg/2 lb ripe tomatoes, peeled, seeded and
    chopped
1 kg/2 lb red and/or green peppers, seeded
    and thinly sliced
2 bay leaves
2 sprigs thyme
4 sprigs parsley
boiled or steamed rice to serve

1. Clean chicken and cut into 8 serving pieces. Melt butter and olive oil in a large flameproof casserole and sauté chicken pieces in amalgamation of fats until golden. Season with paprika, salt and freshly ground black pepper and cayenne, to taste.

2. Add finely chopped onions and garlic, chopped tomatoes, thinly sliced peppers, bay leaves, thyme and parsley. Cook, covered, over a gentle heat, or in a cool oven (150°C, 300°F, Gas Mark 2) for 1½ to 2 hours.

3. To serve: remove herbs and correct seasoning (the dish should be very highly spiced). Serve in casserole accompanied by boiled or steamed rice.

62

Braised Chicken Henri IV

1 tender chicken (about 1.5 kg/3½ lb)
3 level tablespoons butter
3 tablespoons olive oil
6 tablespoons chicken stock
6 tablespoons dry white wine

STUFFING
chicken liver
100 g/4 oz green bacon
225 g/8 oz sausagemeat
2 cloves garlic
100 g/4 oz dried breadcrumbs
milk to moisten
3 level tablespoons finely chopped parsley
½ level teaspoon dried thyme
½ level teaspoon dried tarragon or chervil
generous pinch of mixed spice
2 eggs
salt and freshly ground black pepper

GARNISH
(1) poached vegetables of your choice, or
(2) individual baked tart cases filled with cooked peas, glazed carrots or button onions

1. To make stuffing: put chicken liver, green bacon, sausagemeat and garlic through the finest blade of your mincer. Moisten breadcrumbs with milk, combine with minced meats and add finely chopped parsley, dried herbs, mixed spice, eggs, and salt and freshly ground black pepper, to taste. Mix well, adding more milk if necessary to make fairly loose mixture.

2. Stuff chicken with this mixture; sew up openings and truss bird. Sauté bird in butter and olive oil in a flameproof casserole until golden on all sides. Add stock and dry white wine. Cover casserole and simmer gently for approximately 1 hour, or until tender. If there is any stuffing left over, place it in a small soufflé dish, cover with foil and cook it in the oven.

3. To serve for a family luncheon: Serve braised chicken surrounded by freshly poached vegetables . . . your choice of carrots, turnips, onions, green beans and potatoes.

4. To serve for a dinner party: Place braised chicken on a heated serving dish and surround with individual pastry cases filled with cooked peas, glazed carrots or button onions.

Coq-au-vin à la Beaujolaise

young cock or roasting chicken (about 1.5 kg/3 lb)
3 level tablespoons butter
2 tablespoons olive oil
100 g/4 oz salt pork or unsmoked bacon, diced
12 button onions
12 button mushrooms
seasoned flour
300 ml/½ pint chicken stock (made with a stock cube)
4 tablespoons cognac, warmed
1 sugar lump
1 level tablespoon flour
2 tablespoons finely chopped parsley

MARINADE
2 cloves garlic, chopped
1 large Spanish onion, chopped
1 sprig thyme
2 bay leaves
2 sprigs parsley
½ bottle good Beaujolais
salt and freshly ground black pepper

1. Cut the chicken into serving pieces. Combine marinade ingredients in a large bowl (not metal), add chicken pieces and marinate chicken in this mixture overnight.

2. The following day, melt 2 level tablespoons butter with the olive oil in a flameproof casserole. Add salt pork or bacon, diced, and sauté until golden. Add button onions and cook, stirring, for 3 or 4 minutes; then add mushrooms and sauté the mixture gently until onions begin to turn transparent and mushrooms become brown. Remove pork or bacon, onions and mushrooms from the casserole and keep warm.

3. Remove chicken pieces from the marinade. Pat dry, roll in seasoned flour and sauté them in the same fat for about 5 minutes, or until they turn golden brown on one side. Then, without piercing, turn chicken pieces over to brown on the other side. As each piece begins to 'stiffen', remove it and put in a covered dish in a warm oven.

4. When all of the chicken pieces have been browned, return the onions, bacon, mushrooms, chicken segments and their juices to the casserole. Pour over marinade juices, add chicken stock and bring to the boil. Cover casserole and cook in a moderate oven (180°C, 350°F, Gas Mark 4) for 50 to 60 minutes, until almost tender.

5. Remove chicken pieces, bacon and vegetables from the casserole and keep warm. Skim off excess fat from the juices in casserole. Set casserole on a high heat, pour in cognac, warmed in a soup ladle, and ignite. Allow to burn for a minute or two and then add a lump of sugar. Bring to the boil and reduce the sauce over a high heat to half the original quantity. Thicken with *beurre manié* made of the remaining 1 level tablespoon butter and 1 level tablespoon flour.

6. Strain sauce into a clean casserole; return chicken pieces, bacon and vegetables to the casserole; cover and let simmer in a cool oven (140–150°C, 275–300°F, Gas Mark 1–2) until ready to serve. Garnish with finely chopped parsley.

Pollo alla Romana con Peperoni 63

2 small frying chickens (about 1.25 kg/ 2½ lb each)
salt and freshly ground black pepper
4-6 tablespoons olive oil
½ Spanish onion, finely chopped
300 ml/½ pint dry white wine
450 g/1 lb tomatoes, peeled, seeded and chopped
2 cloves garlic, mashed
2-4 green peppers, sliced

1. Cut chickens into serving pieces and season to taste with salt and freshly ground black pepper.

2. Sauté chicken pieces in olive oil until golden brown on all sides. Add finely chopped onion and dry white wine, and cook over a high heat until wine is reduced to half the original quantity.

3. Add chopped tomatoes and garlic, cover pan and simmer for 20 to 30 minutes, until chicken is tender.

4. In the meantime, sauté sliced green peppers in a little olive oil until tender. Serve with the chicken.

64

Hochepot de Poularde

1 tender chicken (about 1.5 kg/3½ lb)
4-6 tablespoons Calvados (apple brandy)
salt and freshly ground black pepper
4 level tablespoons butter
2 tablespoons olive oil
4 sticks celery, thinly sliced
1 large Spanish onion, thinly sliced
150 ml/¼ pint dry white wine
300 ml/½ pint chicken stock
4 egg yolks
150 ml/¼ pint double cream

GARNISH
4-6 croûtons fried in butter
2 level tablespoons finely chopped parsley

1. Cut chicken into serving pieces and place in a large bowl with Calvados. Season to taste with salt and freshly ground black pepper and allow chicken pieces to marinate in this mixture for at least 4 hours, turning pieces from time to time.

2. Melt butter in a thick-bottomed flameproof casserole; add olive oil and sauté thinly sliced celery and onion over a low heat until vegetables are soft, stirring constantly. Add dry white wine, cover casserole and simmer gently for 10 minutes. Add chicken pieces (reserving marinade juices) and pour over chicken stock. Cover casserole and simmer gently for 50 to 60 minutes, until chicken is tender. Remove chicken pieces from casserole and keep warm.

3. Whisk egg yolks and cream and add to marinade juices. Pour this mixture into casserole and cook over a low heat with juices and vegetables, stirring constantly, until mixture is thick (do not allow mixture to come to the boil, or egg yolks will curdle and sauce will separate).

4. Add chicken pieces to sauce and heat through. Transfer to a heated serving dish, garnish with *croûtons* and sprinkle with finely chopped parsley.

Poularde St. Honoré

1 roasting chicken (about 1.5 kg/3½ lb)

FILLING
225 g/8 oz cooked ham
2-3 level tablespoons tomato purée
4 level tablespoons double cream
paprika
salt and freshly ground black pepper
2-3 drops red food colouring
  (optional)

GARNISH
cooked carrot, truffle, and white
  of hard-boiled egg, cut in
  fancy shapes
Aspic Jelly (see page 90)

1. Roast or cook chicken in a casserole until golden and very tender. When cold, ease the legs away from the body without quite separating them, and carefully remove the flesh from the breast in one long piece on each side. Cut away the upper part of the breast bone with kitchen shears, leaving the chicken quite hollow in the centre, ready for the filling. Lay breast fillets on a board, skin side up, and cut them into slices lengthwise without quite separating the pieces.

2. To make filling: trim ham, removing all gristle and skin, and chop or mince it finely. Pound it well in a mortar with tomato purée. Add cream gradually, until mixture has a creamy consistency, without being too soft. Season to taste with paprika, salt and freshly ground black pepper. Tint lightly with red food colouring if desired.

3. To decorate: fill hollow of the chicken with ham mixture, reforming the whole bird. Lay the breast pieces on each side, separating the slices a little to show some of the white. Decorate the top, where the filling shows, with pieces of cooked carrot, truffle, and white of hard-boiled egg, or any other garnish preferred, covering the filling entirely. Brush over with slightly liquid aspic jelly and allow to set.

4. Serve chicken surrounded with chopped aspic.

Duck en Daube (see page 72)

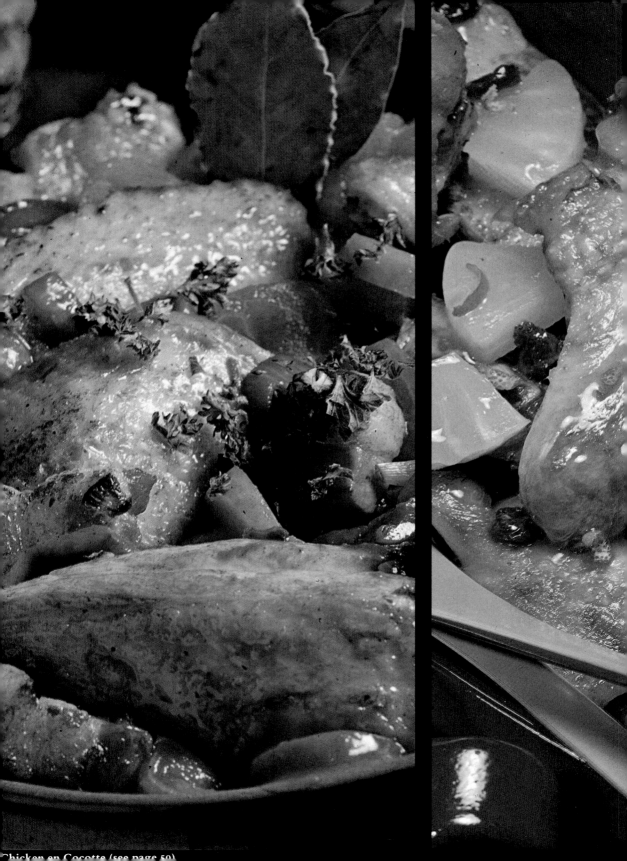

Pineapple Duck (see page 73)   Arroz con Pollo (see page 71)

Moroccan Chicken (see page 69)

Chicken Paprika

2 young chickens (about 1.25 kg/2½ lb each)
salt and freshly ground black pepper
100 g/4 oz butter
1 large Spanish onion, chopped
2 level tablespoons paprika
1 level tablespoon flour
450 ml/¾ pint well-flavoured chicken stock
2 level tablespoons tomato purée
150 ml/¼ pint double cream
juice of ½ lemon

1. Rinse chickens and pat dry. Cut into serving pieces and season with salt and freshly ground black pepper.

2. Heat butter in a flameproof casserole or large iron frying pan, add onion and cook until transparent. Stir in paprika. Add chicken and cook slowly until pieces are golden, then reduce heat, cover casserole and simmer gently for 20 minutes longer, or until chicken is almost tender. Sprinkle with flour, add stock and tomato purée, stir well and cover. Bring to the boil and simmer for 20 minutes.

3. Remove chicken to a warmed serving dish.

4. Add cream and lemon juice to casserole, stir well and cook for 5 minutes. Correct seasoning and pour sauce over chicken.

Italian Chicken with Sausages

2 tablespoons olive oil
1 Spanish onion, sliced
2 cloves garlic, sliced
50 g/2 oz mushrooms, sliced
4 negroni or 8 chipolata sausages
1 chicken (about 2.25 kg/5 lb)
1 425-g/15-oz) can Italian peeled tomatoes
2 tablespoons tomato purée
6 tablespoons red wine
salt and freshly ground black pepper

1. Heat olive oil in a thick-bottomed pan. Sauté onion and garlic until transparent. Add mushrooms and sauté until golden. Set aside.

2. Sauté sausages in fat remaining in pan until golden. Remove, allow to cool and slice in 5-cm/2-inch segments.

3. Cut chicken into serving pieces and brown in the fat. Return onion, garlic, mushrooms and sausages to the pan. Add tomatoes and tomato purée, and simmer gently for at least 45 minutes.

4. Add the wine and cook for 5 minutes longer. Season with salt and freshly ground black pepper.

Moroccan Chicken
Illustrated opposite

1 chicken (1.75-2.25 kg/4-5 lb)
salt
¼ level teaspoon paprika
¼ level teaspoon powdered cumin
freshly ground black pepper
butter
350 g/12 oz Spanish onions, sliced
⅛-¼ level teaspoon powdered saffron
100 g/4 oz chick peas, soaked overnight
well-flavoured chicken stock
4 tablespoons finely chopped parsley
1 sprig fresh coriander or lemon thyme
225 g/8 oz rice
lemon juice

1. Cut chicken into serving pieces and season to taste with salt, paprika, powdered cumin and freshly ground black pepper. Sauté chicken pieces with sliced onions in 75 g/3 oz butter in a casserole until golden.

2. Sprinkle with powdered saffron; add chick peas and enough well-flavoured chicken stock to cover, and simmer gently for 1 to 1½ hours, until chicken is tender. Just before serving, add chopped parsley and coriander or lemon thyme.

3. Cook the rice in salted water with 2 tablespoons butter.

4. **To serve:** spoon half the rice into a heated serving dish, place chicken pieces on it and pour over saffron sauce. Add remaining rice and sprinkle with lemon juice.

70

Poularde au Porto

1 plump chicken (about 1.5 kg/3½ lb)
4–6 level tablespoons butter
225 g/8 oz mushroom caps
4 tablespoons cognac
400 ml/14 fl oz double cream
4–6 tablespoons port
1 level tablespoon cornflour
salt and freshly ground black pepper

1. Cut chicken into 4 serving pieces and simmer gently in butter for 10 minutes, turning pieces from time to time so that chicken does not brown. Add mushroom caps, cover pan and continue cooking until tender, turning chicken pieces from time to time.

2. Place chicken and mushrooms on a hot serving dish and keep warm.

3. Add cognac to pan, stirring well to scrape all crusty bits from sides of the pan. Stir in cream and port, mixed with cornflour, and continue cooking over a high heat until sauce is reduced to half the original quantity. Correct seasoning and pour sauce over chicken and mushrooms. Serve immediately.

Poulet du Marquis

2 small chickens (about 1 kg/2 lb each)
2 rashers bacon, cut in half
salt and freshly ground black pepper
4 tablespoons cognac
300 ml/½ pint double cream
1 egg yolk
2 level tablespoons butter

1. Truss birds, cover breasts with rashers of bacon and place in a thick-bottomed flameproof casserole. Season to taste with salt and freshly ground black pepper. Roast in a moderately hot oven (190°C, 375°F, Gas Mark 5) for 30 to 40 minutes, until breasts are tender when pierced with a fork.

2. Remove birds from casserole and slice off breast meat in single pieces. Keep warm.

3. Remove remaining meat from carcasses and chop finely. Chop bones coarsely. Add chopped meat and bones to casserole and simmer gently for 5 to 10 minutes, stirring from time to time. Skim off fat and add 2 tablespoons cognac and flame.

4. Whisk cream and egg yolk together and pour into casserole. Cook sauce gently, stirring continuously, until slightly thickened. Do not allow sauce to come to the boil or it will curdle.

5. Finish sauce by whisking in remaining cognac and butter. Correct seasoning and strain sauce through a colander (to remove bones) on to chicken breasts. Serve immediately.

Egyptian Lemon Chicken

2 small chickens (about 1.25 kg/2½ lb each)
4 tablespoons olive oil
1 clove garlic, finely chopped
grated rind and juice of 1 lemon
¼ level teaspoon dried thyme
salt and freshly ground black pepper
100 g/4 oz butter
2 level tablespoons finely chopped parsley

1. Cut chickens into serving pieces and place in a shallow bowl.

2. Sprinkle with olive oil, finely chopped garlic, grated rind and juice of 1 lemon, and thyme, and season to taste with salt and freshly ground black pepper. Marinate chicken pieces in this mixture for at least 2 hours, turning pieces from time to time.

3. When ready to cook, butter a rectangular ovenproof baking dish generously. Place chicken pieces and juices in dish and dot with butter. Cook in a moderate oven (190°C, 350°F, Gas Mark 4) for 50 to 60 minutes, until tender, basting frequently. When tender, remove from oven, sprinkle with finely chopped parsley, and serve immediately.

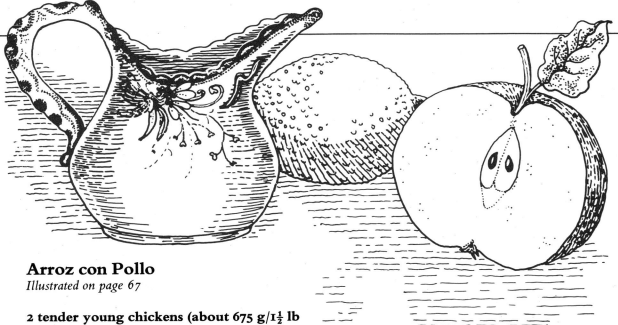

Arroz con Pollo
Illustrated on page 67

2 tender young chickens (about 675 g/1½ lb
  each)
salt and freshly ground black pepper
8 tablespoons olive oil
½ Spanish onion, finely chopped
1 clove garlic, finely chopped
6 tablespoons well-flavoured Italian
   Tomato Sauce (see page 91)
⅛ level teaspoon powdered saffron
2 canned pimientos, sliced
600 ml/1 pint well-flavoured chicken stock
175 g/6 oz rice
grated rind of ½ lemon
2 tablespoons freshly chopped parsley

1. Cut each chicken into serving portions, season, and sauté in olive oil until golden on all sides. Stir in finely chopped onion and garlic, and continue to cook until onion is soft. **Note:** do not let onion go brown.

2. Add Italian Tomato Sauce, saffron, sliced pimientos and chicken stock; cover saucepan and simmer for 15 minutes.

3. Stir rice into chicken and vegetable mixture and season with salt and freshly ground black pepper. Cover saucepan again and simmer for 30 minutes, or until all the liquids have been absorbed and the chicken is tender.

4. Sprinkle with grated lemon rind and chopped parsley, and serve immediately.

Curried Chicken

2 level tablespoons butter
2 tablespoons olive oil
1 Spanish onion, finely chopped
2 sticks celery, thinly sliced
2 cloves garlic, finely chopped
1–2 level tablespoons curry powder
2 level tablespoons flour
300 ml/½ pint chicken stock
150 ml/¼ pint dry white wine
675 g/1½ lb cooked chicken, diced
1–2 cooking apples (according to size),
  peeled, cored and diced
3 level tablespoons finely chopped parsley
cooked rice

1. Melt butter and oil and sauté finely chopped Spanish onion and sliced celery until onion is transparent. Add finely chopped garlic and curry powder mixed with flour and continue to cook, stirring constantly, until mixture begins to turn golden.

2. Stir in stock and white wine, and cook the sauce, stirring, until it is smooth and thick.

3. Add diced chicken, apple and finely chopped parsley, and simmer until heated through. Serve curried chicken in a ring of cooked rice.

72

Duck with Garlic

2 large cloves garlic, crushed
2 level teaspoons salt
1 level teaspoon freshly ground black pepper
1 level teaspoon paprika
1 tender duckling, cut into serving pieces
4 tablespoons olive oil
2 Spanish onions, finely chopped
2 bay leaves
1 strip dried orange peel

1. Mash garlic with salt to a paste; add freshly ground black pepper and paprika. Rub duck pieces on all sides with this aromatic paste.

2. Heat oil in the bottom of a flameproof casserole. Sauté onions in it until transparent. Remove onions from casserole with a slotted spoon and sauté duck pieces in remaining fat until golden on all sides.

3. Return onions to casserole; add 2 bay leaves and a strip of dried orange peel and simmer duck, covered, in a cool oven (150°C, 300°F, Gas Mark 2) for 40 to 50 minutes, until tender.

Duck en Daube
Illustrated on page 65

1 tender duck
salt and freshly ground black pepper
1 stick celery, chopped
2 carrots, sliced
2 large onions, sliced
8 tablespoons cognac
450 ml/¾ pint dry red wine
100 g/4 oz fat bacon, diced
1 tablespoon olive oil
1 bouquet garni (marjoram, 1 stick celery, 2 sprigs parsley)
1 clove garlic
225 g/8 oz mushrooms, sliced

1. Cut duck into serving pieces and place in a porcelain or earthenware bowl. Add salt and freshly ground black pepper, celery, carrots, sliced onions, cognac and red wine; marinate the duck in this mixture for at least 2 hours.

2. Remove duck pieces from the marinade; drain and dry with a clean cloth.

3. Sauté diced bacon in olive oil until golden. Remove bacon bits, and brown duck pieces in fat. Place bacon bits and duck pieces with pan juices in a large ovenproof casserole, cover, and simmer gently for 20 minutes.

4. Add the marinade, *bouquet garni*, garlic and mushrooms. Simmer over a very low heat for 1½ hours, or until duck is tender. Remove *bouquet garni*, skim fat and correct seasoning.

5. Serve from the casserole.

Duck with Turnips

1 tender duck (1.75 kg/4 lb)
salt
2 level tablespoons flour
freshly ground black pepper
4 level tablespoons butter
4-8 young turnips, quartered
1 level tablespoon castor sugar
900 ml/1½ pints well-flavoured stock
1 bouquet garni (marjoram, sage, 2 sprigs parsley)
1 Spanish onion, quartered

1. To prepare duck: singe and draw the duck, making a slit lengthwise above the vent to facilitate pulling out the inside. Then wash the bird quickly in warm water and dry it in a cloth. Cut off the feet and wings at the first joint, and rub the bird with salt inside and out.

2. To truss duck: lay the bird on its back and turn the wings under. Bring the legs close to the body and pass a metal or wooden skewer first through flesh of the wing, the middle of the leg and the body, then out the other side through the other leg and the wing. Pass a piece of string over each end of the skewer, bring it round the vent, fasten the legs tightly and tie securely.

73

3. Dust duck with 1 tablespoon flour and season inside and out with freshly ground black pepper.

4. Melt butter in a flameproof casserole and sauté duck on all sides until it is nicely browned.

5. Remove the duck and add quartered turnips to juices in the casserole. Sprinkle with sugar and simmer turnips until lightly coloured. Remove and keep warm.

6. Stir remaining flour into the fat left in the casserole until smooth, and pour in the stock. Bring to the boil and skim. Add *bouquet garni* and quartered onion, and season to taste.

7. Return duck to casserole, cover and cook gently for 1½ hours. Add turnips and continue cooking about 30 to 40 minutes longer, until the duck and turnips are tender, turning duck occasionally during cooking time.

8. When ready to serve: transfer duck to a hot serving dish, remove strings, and arrange turnips around duck. Skim fat from pan juices, reduce over a high heat, and strain over and round the duck.

Pineapple Duck
Illustrated on page 67

1 duck, cut into serving pieces
olive oil
1 (425-g/15-oz) can pineapple slices with juice
1 glass red wine
1 clove garlic, finely chopped
salt and freshly ground black pepper

PINEAPPLE AND ORANGE SAUCE
15 g/½ oz cornflour
juice and grated rind of 1 orange
juices from the duck, made up to 300 ml/ ½ pint with water
50 g/2 oz seedless raisins

1. Place the duck, cut into serving pieces, in a roasting tin and brush well with olive oil. Pour the juices from the can of pineapple into the tin

with the red wine, finely chopped garlic, and salt and freshly ground black pepper, to taste. Cook in a moderately hot oven (190°C, 375°F, Gas Mark 5) for 40 minutes, or until thoroughly cooked. Baste frequently with the juices.

2. To make Pineapple and Orange Sauce: mix cornflour to a smooth paste with orange juice. Heat pan juices, skimmed of fat and made up to 300 ml/½ pint with water, and pour over the cornflour mixture. Return to the roasting tin and cook until thick. Add chopped pineapple slices, raisins and grated orange rind, and heat through.

3. Serve duck with Pineapple and Orange Sauce.

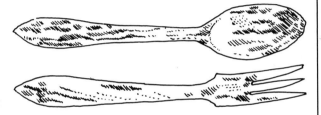

Malay Duck

2 level tablespoons coriander seeds, roasted in a dry pan
1 level teaspoon black peppercorns
2 level tablespoons honey
2 tablespoons soy sauce
salt
1 tender duckling, prepared
1 Spanish onion, finely chopped
4 tablespoons peanut oil
450 ml/¾ pint hot chicken stock
cinnamon and cloves

1. Pound 'roasted' coriander and black peppercorns in a mortar until powdered. Add honey, soy sauce, and salt, to taste, and rub mixture into duck, inside and out.

2. Sauté finely chopped onion in peanut oil until soft and transparent in a flameproof casserole. Add the duck and sauté it until golden on all sides. Then add chicken stock, and cinnamon and cloves, to taste. Simmer for 1½ hours, or until duckling is tender and there is little sauce left.

Canard Braisé à l'Orange

1 tender duck (2.25–2.75 kg/5–6 lb)
salt and freshly ground black pepper
6–8 level tablespoons butter
150 ml/¼ pint Cointreau
4 oranges
1 level tablespoon sugar
1 tablespoon vinegar
150 ml/¼ pint beef stock
watercress

1. Trim wingtips and cut off the neck of duck. Wipe the bird with a damp clean cloth inside and out, and sprinkle the cavity with salt and freshly ground black pepper.

2. Melt butter in a deep flameproof casserole just large enough to contain duck, and sauté duck until golden on all sides. Reduce heat, cover and simmer gently for 45 minutes, turning duck from time to time. Add two-thirds of the Cointreau and allow to simmer for a few more minutes.

3. In the meantime, peel 1 orange thinly. Then cut the rind into thin slivers. Reserve rind for later use. Peel remaining 3 oranges and cut into segments. Reserve segments for garnish.

4. Remove duck and keep warm. Add sugar, vinegar, juice of remaining peeled orange and beef stock to pan juices. Place casserole over a high heat and bring to the boil, stirring constantly, scraping all the crusty bits from sides of casserole into sauce. Add slivered orange rind, reduce heat to lowest possible, and simmer sauce gently for 10 minutes.

5. Skim fat from surface and pass sauce through a fine sieve. Season generously with salt and freshly ground black pepper, and add remaining Cointreau. (Sauce may be thickened if desired.)

6. Place half the orange segments in a saucepan, strain sauce over them and bring to the boil. Remove from heat.

7. To serve: place duck on heated serving dish, pour a little sauce around it and garnish with remaining fresh orange segments and sprigs of watercress. Serve orange sauce separately.

Cold Jellied Duck en Casserole

1 tender duckling, prepared
salt and freshly ground black pepper
butter
150 ml/¼ pint dry white wine
600 ml/1 pint chicken stock
1 bouquet garni (2 sprigs parsley,
 2 sprigs thyme, 1 stick celery,
 2 bay leaves)
100 g/4 oz fat bacon, cut into cubes
12 young turnips
12 button mushrooms
12 button onions
4 level tablespoons minced raw beef
2 egg shells, crushed
2 egg whites, beaten
2 level tablespoons gelatine

1. Wipe the duckling with a damp clean cloth inside and out and season generously with salt and freshly ground black pepper, both the cavity and the outside of the duckling. Sauté in 4 level tablespoons butter in a flameproof casserole until bird is golden on all sides. Moisten with dry white wine, bring to the boil and add chicken stock. Add salt, freshly ground black pepper and a *bouquet garni*.

2. Sauté bacon cubes in 2 level tablespoons butter until golden. Remove and sauté turnips in resulting fat until golden.

3. Combine sautéed bacon and turnips with button mushrooms and onions and add to duckling. Simmer, covered, for about 1½ hours, until duckling is tender and vegetables are cooked through, basting duckling from time to time.

4. Remove duckling, cut it into serving pieces and place pieces in a small oval casserole (or terrine) just large enough to hold it. Surround with bacon cubes, turnips, mushrooms and onions.

5. Strain stock through a sieve into a bowl; cool and remove fat from surface.

6. Clarify the stock by bringing it to the boil with minced raw beef, crushed egg shells and beaten egg whites. Strain, while hot, through a sieve lined with a wet flannel cloth. Soften gelatine in a little cold water, stir into the hot stock and pour over duckling, which should be covered. If not, add a little more water, stock and wine. Allow to set for 12 hours before serving. Serve with a tossed green salad.

Hungarian Duck

1 Spanish onion, finely chopped
100 g/4 oz cooked ham, chopped
2 rashers bacon, chopped
olive oil
8 level tablespoons cooked rice
4 level tablespoons finely chopped parsley
1 egg, well beaten
6 level tablespoons soured cream
salt and freshly ground black pepper
1 tender duckling, prepared
2 level tablespoons butter
450 g/1 lb tomatoes, peeled and quartered
2 small aubergines, quartered
2 small green peppers, seeded and quartered
2 Spanish onions, quartered
6 tablespoons dry white wine

1. Sauté finely chopped onion, ham and bacon in a little olive oil until onion is transparent. Combine with cooked rice, finely chopped parsley, well-beaten egg and soured cream and season generously with salt and freshly ground black pepper.

2. Stuff duckling loosely with this mixture and brown bird on all sides in 2 tablespoons each olive oil and butter in a flameproof casserole. Add quartered tomatoes, aubergines, green peppers and onions, moisten with 6 tablespoons each dry white wine and olive oil and season with salt and freshly ground black pepper, to taste. Cover casserole and cook in a moderate oven (160°C, 325°F, Gas Mark 3) for about 2 hours. Serve from the casserole.

76

Turkey à la King

butter
2 level tablespoons flour
½ chicken stock cube
300 ml/½ pint double cream
salt and freshly ground black pepper
675 g/1½ lb cooked turkey, cut into cubes
2 canned pimientos, cut into cubes
1 green pepper, cut into cubes
6 black olives
2 level tablespoons finely chopped parsley

1. Melt 2 level tablespoons butter in the top of a double saucepan over direct heat. Add flour and cook, stirring constantly, until the *roux* is well blended. Then stir in ½ chicken stock cube and double cream and cook over simmering water, stirring from time to time, until sauce is smooth and thick. Season with salt and freshly ground black pepper.

2. Butter an ovenproof casserole generously. Spread cubed turkey in the bottom of casserole. Add cubed pimientos and green pepper to cream sauce and pour over turkey.

3. Cook in a moderate oven (180°C, 350°F, Gas Mark 4) for 25 to 30 minutes. Garnish with a ring of black olives and a sprinkle of finely chopped parsley and serve immediately.

Guinea Fowl en Cocotte

1 large cooking apple, coarsely grated
1 Spanish onion, coarsely grated
1 (85-g/3-oz) packet Philadelphia cream
   cheese, mashed
6 juniper berries, crushed
lemon juice
salt and freshly ground black pepper
2 guinea fowl
butter
olive oil
150 ml/¼ pint dry white wine

1. Combine apple and onion with mashed cream cheese, crushed juniper berries, and lemon juice, salt and freshly ground black pepper, to taste.

2. Stuff birds with this mixture. Skewer openings and truss birds; spread with well-seasoned softened butter.

3. Place birds in a flameproof casserole and sauté in a little butter and olive oil until golden on all sides. Lower heat and add dry white wine. Cover casserole and simmer birds gently, turning them from time to time, until tender – about 45 to 60 minutes.

Pintade Roti aux Poires

2 Spanish onions, finely chopped
100 g/4 oz butter
2 small guinea fowl
salt and freshly ground black pepper
8 pears, peeled, cored and halved
100 g/4 oz sugar
300 ml/½ pint water
juice of 1 lemon
1 strip of lemon peel
150 ml/¼ pint dry white wine
150 ml/¼ pint port
boiled rice to serve

1. Sauté finely chopped onions in butter in a flameproof casserole until transparent. Remove onions from casserole with a slotted spoon and

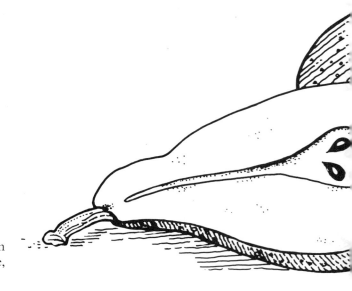

reserve. Sauté dressed guinea fowl in the butter until golden on all sides.

2. Return onions to casserole, season generously with salt and freshly ground black pepper and cook at medium heat, covered, turning guinea fowl from time to time.

3. Poach halved pears in a syrup of sugar, water, half the lemon juice and strip of lemon peel, until just tender. When the birds are half cooked (15 to 20 minutes), add halved pears, 8 tablespoons of the syrup, dry white wine and port to the casserole. Simmer for a further 15 to 20 minutes at the same heat, until guinea fowl are tender. Add salt, freshly ground black pepper and a little lemon juice, to taste.

4. To serve: cut guinea fowl into quarters, cover each quarter with a halved pear and coat with the strained reduced sauce. Serve with rice.

Herbed Guinea Fowl

2 small guinea fowl
2 cloves garlic, finely chopped
½ level teaspoon dried thyme
butter
grated rind of ¼ lemon
lemon juice
salt and freshly ground black pepper

1. Cut guinea fowl into quarters.

2. Pound garlic, thyme, 6 tablespoons softened butter and lemon rind to a smooth paste with lemon juice and salt and freshly ground black pepper, to taste.

3. Rub birds inside and out with this mixture. Place in a well-buttered shallow casserole dish and cook in a moderately hot oven (190°C, 375°F, Gas Mark 5) for 35 to 45 minutes, until tender.

Game

Pheasant Soubise *Serves 4 to 8, according to size of birds*
Faisan aux Fruits *Serves 4 to 6*
Casseroled Pheasant in Red Wine *Serves 4 to 6*

78

Pheasant Soubise

2 plump pheasants
4 rashers streaky bacon, or thinly pounded
  pork fat
225 g/8 oz green bacon, in 1 piece
4 level tablespoons butter
2 tablespoons olive oil
2 Spanish onions, finely chopped
600 ml/1 pint single cream
salt and freshly ground black pepper

1. Clean and truss pheasants and cover breasts with bacon rashers or thinly pounded pork fat.

2. Dice green bacon and sauté in butter and olive oil in a flameproof casserole until golden. Remove and sauté finely chopped onions in resulting fats until transparent. Remove and sauté pheasants gently until they are golden on all sides. Return onions and bacon to casserole with pheasants, add cream and season generously with salt and freshly ground black pepper. Cover casserole and simmer gently for about 1 hour, until pheasants are tender.

3. To serve: transfer pheasants and bacon bits to a hot serving dish. Purée cream sauce in an electric blender (or force through a fine sieve) and pour over pheasants.

Faisan aux Fruits

2 fat pheasants
4 level tablespoons butter
salt and freshly ground black pepper
4 tablespoons cognac
2 tablespoons game fumet (see method,
  Step 2)
2 tablespoons lemon juice
2 tablespoons pineapple juice
4 slices fresh pineapple, halved
1 orange, peeled and cut in segments

1. To prepare birds: cut each bird into 8 serving pieces and sauté the wings, breasts and thighs in butter until golden. (Keep the drumsticks for another use; they are excellent devilled.) Season well with salt and freshly ground black pepper,

and continue to cook until pheasant is tender. Remove pieces and keep warm.

2. To make fruit sauce: remove half the fat in the pan, add cognac and set alight. Then bring to the boil, stirring briskly to dissolve crusty bits on side of pan. Add a little *fumet* of game (made by boiling neck, carcass and giblets of birds for a minute or two in a very little water with finely chopped onion, salt and pepper), then add lemon juice and pineapple juice.

3. Arrange pieces of pheasant on a warm serving dish, garnish with pineapple and orange segments and pour over sauce.

Casseroled Pheasant in Red Wine
Illustrated on page 88

2 young pheasants
olive oil
salt and freshly ground black pepper
8 level tablespoons finely chopped Spanish
  onion
3 level tablespoons butter
600 ml/1 pint red Burgundy
1 level tablespoon flour

SAUTÉED MUSHROOM CAPS
12-16 button mushrooms
2 level tablespoons butter
2 tablespoons lemon juice
$\frac{1}{4}$ level teaspoon thyme
salt and freshly ground black pepper

1. Clean birds; brush with olive oil and season generously inside and out with salt and freshly ground black pepper. Put 2 level tablespoons finely chopped onion and the pheasant liver into the cavity of each bird.

2. Heat 2 tablespoons olive oil and 2 level tablespoons butter in a large thick pan and sauté pheasants gently until they are a golden brown colour on all sides and almost tender. Transfer pheasants to a large ovenproof casserole and keep warm.

3. Pour red wine into pan in which you have

cooked birds and cook over a high heat, amalgamating wine with the pan juices. Add remaining finely chopped onion and continue to cook, stirring, until the liquid is reduced by half. Thicken the sauce with the remaining butter and flour. Simmer for a few minutes, strain through a fine sieve into a bowl and allow to cool slightly so that fat can be skimmed off the surface.

4. To cook mushroom caps: sauté button mushrooms in butter and lemon juice with thyme. Season to taste with salt and freshly ground black pepper. Keep warm.

5. Pour wine sauce over the pheasants, correct seasoning and add sautéed mushrooms. Cover casserole and cook in a moderately hot oven (190°C, 375°F, Gas Mark 5) for about 45 minutes, until pheasants are tender.

Grouse en Cocotte

2 tender grouse
fat bacon
salt and freshly ground black pepper
2 level tablespoons butter
2 tablespoons olive oil
4 shallots, coarsely chopped
2 carrots, coarsely chopped
2 tablespoons cognac
1 bouquet garni (2 sprigs parsley, 2 sprigs thyme, 1 bay leaf)
150 ml/¼ pint red wine
150 ml/¼ pint well-flavoured stock

1. Ask your poulterer to prepare birds for roasting.

2. Place a layer of fat bacon over breasts. Season birds with salt and freshly ground black pepper, to taste.

3. Heat butter and oil in an iron *cocotte* or a heavy flameproof casserole, and sauté 100 g/4 oz diced fat bacon until golden.

4. Remove bacon pieces and reserve. Add chopped shallots and carrots to the casserole and cook, stirring constantly, until vegetables soften. Then add grouse and brown well on all sides.

5. Return bacon pieces to the casserole, pour over cognac, and flame. Then add *bouquet garni*, red wine and well-flavoured stock. Cover the casserole and let the birds simmer over a low heat for 30 minutes, or until tender. Add more wine or stock if the sauce reduces too quickly while cooking.

Salmis of Grouse

3 grouse
6 tablespoons red or dry white wine
6 tablespoons rich beef stock
2 lemons
salt and freshly ground black pepper
freshly grated nutmeg
1–2 level tablespoons dry mustard
65 g/2½ oz mushrooms, sliced
1 level tablespoon butter
1 level tablespoon flour
2 level tablespoons finely chopped parsley

1. Roast grouse slightly in a moderately hot oven (200°C, 400°F, Gas Mark 6) for 15 to 20 minutes, until about half cooked. Cut them into serving pieces. Be sure to cut birds on a carving dish to catch blood and juices. Arrange pieces in a large shallow flameproof casserole.

2. Crush livers and giblets into a bowl with juices. Add red or dry white wine, beef stock and juice of 2 lemons; stir in the finely grated peel of 1 lemon and season to taste with salt, freshly ground black pepper, nutmeg and mustard.

3. Add sliced mushrooms and pour this mixture over the birds in the casserole. Cook until heated through, stirring so that each piece of meat is thoroughly moistened and is kept from sticking to the dish. Do not let the *salmis* come to the boil.

4. Just before serving, stir in a *beurre manié* made of equal quantities of butter and flour. Sprinkle with finely chopped parsley.

80

Pigeons with Green Peas

2 young pigeons
4 level tablespoons butter
8–10 small white onions, peeled
100 g/4 oz bacon, diced
1 level tablespoon flour
300 ml/½ pint chicken stock
225 g/8 oz peas, fresh or frozen
1 bouquet garni (2 sprigs parsley, 2 sprigs thyme, 1 bay leaf)
salt and freshly ground black pepper

1. Clean and truss pigeons as for roasting.

2. Melt butter in a flameproof casserole and sauté pigeons, turning them over and over until browned on all sides.

3. Remove pigeons, add onions and diced bacon to the casserole, and sauté until golden. Sprinkle with flour and when flour has combined with the butter, add stock and stir until mixture boils.

4. Skim well and return pigeons to the sauce. Add green peas and *bouquet garni*. Season to taste with salt and freshly ground black pepper, cover and simmer gently until the pigeons are tender.

5. Transfer pigeons to the centre of a hot serving dish and surround with peas and onions.

Pigeons with Green Olives

2 young pigeons
4 level tablespoons butter
4 shallots, finely chopped
½ Spanish onion, finely chopped
100 g/4 oz unsmoked bacon, diced
1 level tablespoon flour
300 ml/½ pint chicken stock
2 level tablespoons finely chopped parsley
salt and freshly ground black pepper
thyme and marjoram
16 green olives, stoned, blanched and soaked overnight in cold water and cognac
4 tablespoons cognac

1. Clean and truss the pigeons as for roasting.

2. Melt the butter in a flameproof casserole and sauté the pigeons, turning them over and over until browned on all sides.

3. Remove pigeons, add finely chopped shallots and onion with diced unsmoked bacon to casserole, and sauté until golden. Sprinkle with flour and when flour has combined with the butter, add stock and stir until mixture comes to the boil.

4. Skim well and return pigeons to the sauce. Add finely chopped parsley, and salt, freshly ground black pepper, thyme and marjoram, to taste. Cover casserole and simmer gently for about 2 hours, or until pigeons are tender.

5. Twenty minutes before pigeons are done, add blanched and soaked green olives. Remove cover and continue cooking.

6. To serve: arrange pigeons on a hot serving dish, surround with olives, and strain sauce over.

Pigeons in Red Wine

2 young pigeons
4 level tablespoons butter
1 Spanish onion, finely chopped
1 level tablespoon flour
300 ml/½ pint red wine
1 level teaspoon sugar
1 bouquet garni (2 sprigs thyme, 2 sprigs parsley, 1 bay leaf)
salt and freshly ground black pepper
12 button mushrooms, sautéed in lemon juice and butter
12 small white onions, simmered in red wine and a little sugar
2 level tablespoons finely chopped parsley

1. Clean pigeons and cut them in half.

2. Melt butter in a large, thick-bottomed, flameproof casserole and sauté pigeons until well browned.

3. Remove pigeons from casserole and sauté finely chopped Spanish onion until golden brown. Return pigeons to casserole and sprinkle lightly with flour. When the flour is thoroughly mixed with the butter, add red wine, sugar and *bouquet garni*, and salt and freshly ground black pepper, to taste. Cover casserole and cook in a moderate oven (160°C, 325°F, Gas Mark 3) for 2 hours.

4. Fifteen minutes before serving, add cooked button mushrooms and onions to casserole.

5. When ready to serve, correct seasoning and sprinkle with finely chopped parsley. Serve from the casserole.

Salmis of Wild Duck

2 wild ducks
salt and freshly ground black pepper
dried thyme
8 rashers bacon
300 ml/½ pint port
1 Spanish onion, finely chopped
4 shallots, finely chopped
2 cloves
bouquet garni (4 sprigs parsley, 2 sprigs
   thyme, bay leaf)
300 ml/½ pint red Bordeaux
450 ml/¾ pint Brown Sauce (see page 90)
8 triangular croûtons, sautéed in butter

1. Clean, pluck and singe wild ducks. Rub cavities with salt, freshly ground black pepper and dried thyme. Place ducks, breast sides up, on rack in roasting tins. Cover breasts with bacon and pour port into tins. Roast ducks in a hot oven (230°C, 450°F, Gas Mark 8) for 20 minutes, basting several times with port.

2. Remove bacon, baste well with pan juices and continue roasting until ducks are cooked rare.

3. Cut breasts, wings and legs from ducks; remove skin and place pieces in a flameproof shallow casserole or chafing dish.

4. In a saucepan combine finely chopped onion and shallots, cloves, *bouquet garni*, bones, skins and trimmings from ducks, and red wine. Cook over a high heat until wine is reduced to half the original quantity. Add Brown Sauce, and salt and freshly ground black pepper, to taste; simmer gently for 20 minutes.

5. Strain sauce over duck pieces and simmer on top of the cooker or in a chafing dish at the table until duck is heated through. Garnish with *croûtons* and serve immediately.

Casseroled Partridge

2 small partridges
4 tablespoons melted butter
2 tablespoons olive oil
salt and freshly ground black pepper
2 slices of white bread, trimmed of crusts
4 level tablespoons finely chopped ham
4-6 juniper berries, crushed
grated rind of ½ lemon
marjoram
fat salt pork
6 tablespoons dry white wine
150 ml/¼ pint rich chicken stock
1 carrot, finely chopped
1 small onion, finely chopped

1. Clean partridges inside and out. Brush cavities with half the melted butter, and the olive oil and season liberally with salt and freshly ground black pepper.

2. Shred bread and combine with remaining melted butter, chopped ham, crushed juniper berries and grated lemon rind. Season to taste with salt, freshly ground black pepper and marjoram, and stuff birds loosely with this mixture.

3. Truss birds, wrap a thin piece of fat salt pork around each one and sauté birds in a flameproof casserole until golden on all sides. Add dry white wine, chicken stock, and finely chopped carrot and onion. Transfer casserole to a moderately hot oven (190°C, 375°F, Gas Mark 5) and roast, uncovered, basting birds from time to time, for 45 to 60 minutes, until tender.

82

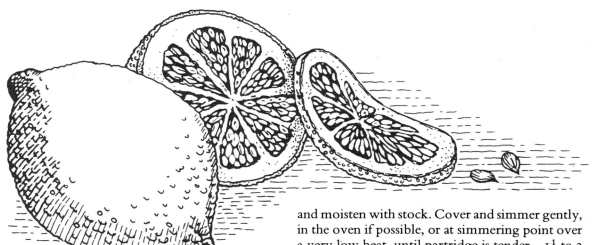

and moisten with stock. Cover and simmer gently, in the oven if possible, or at simmering point over a very low heat, until partridge is tender – $1\frac{1}{2}$ to 2 hours.

5. To serve: remove the partridge, ham and sausages from the saucepan. Cut the partridge into neat joints, and slice the ham and sausages. Remove the carrot, onion and *bouquet garni*. Arrange cabbage on a hot serving dish; place the partridge pieces on top, and garnish with sliced ham and sausages.

Partridge with Cabbage

2 small cabbages
salt
100 g/4 oz ham or lean bacon
2 level tablespoons butter or dripping
1 partridge (over 1 year old), trussed
2 large carrots, coarsely chopped
1 Spanish onion
1–2 cloves
1 bouquet garni (2 sprigs parsley, 2 sprigs
   thyme, 1 bay leaf)
2 small smoked sausages
freshly ground black pepper
well-flavoured stock

1. Trim the cabbages, cut in pieces and wash well. Cook cabbage in boiling salted water for 10 to 12 minutes. Then strain and press out the water.

2. Blanch ham or bacon for a few minutes to remove some of the salt.

3. Melt butter or dripping in a flameproof casserole, put in the partridge, trussed as for roasting, and brown it on all sides.

4. Remove partridge, add half the cabbage with the chopped carrots, the onion stuck with the cloves, and a *bouquet garni*. Lay the partridge, ham and sausages on top, and cover with remaining cabbage. Season with freshly ground black pepper

Stuffed Game Casserole

2 partridges or pheasants
100 g/4 oz lean veal, finely chopped
100 g/4 oz lean ham, finely chopped
6 tablespoons cognac
salt and freshly ground black pepper
$\frac{1}{4}$ level teaspoon each thyme, nutmeg and
   crushed juniper berries
fat salt pork or fat bacon
4 level tablespoons butter
2 tablespoons olive oil
2 shallots, finely chopped
450 g/1 lb button mushrooms
1–2 cloves garlic, finely chopped
juice of $\frac{1}{2}$ lemon

1. Clean partridges and stuff with the following mixture: finely chopped livers and hearts of the birds combined with finely chopped veal and ham, moistened with cognac and flavoured with salt, freshly ground black pepper, thyme, nutmeg and crushed juniper berries.

2. Truss birds firmly and wrap each one in fat salt pork or a slice of fat bacon. Place in a flameproof casserole with 2 tablespoons butter, the olive oil and finely chopped shallots. Cover casserole and simmer partridges for 1 to 1½ hours, until tender.

3. Sauté mushrooms in remaining butter with finely chopped garlic cloves. Season well and pour over partridges. Cover casserole and keep warm on an asbestos mat on top of the cooker or in a cool oven (150°C, 300°F, Gas Mark 2).

Venison en Casserole

1.25 kg/2½ lb venison
100 g/4 oz bacon, in 1 piece
2 level tablespoons flour
450 ml/¾ pint stock or water
1 Spanish onion, finely chopped
2-4 level tablespoons redcurrant jelly
1 bouquet garni (2 sprigs parsley, 2 sprigs
   thyme, 1 bay leaf)
2 tablespoons lemon juice
salt and freshly ground black pepper

FORCEMEAT BALLS
225 g/8 oz sausagemeat
1 egg, beaten
dried herbs

1. Choose a nice fleshy piece of venison; wipe it and trim it carefully and cut it into 2.5-cm/1-inch cubes.

2. Trim rind from bacon and cut it into rectangles. Sauté bacon gently for a few minutes in a frying pan without allowing them to become too brown and crisp. Transfer bacon to a flameproof casserole, leaving the liquid fat in the pan.

3. Coat the pieces of venison with flour and sauté in bacon fat until well browned. Transfer venison to the casserole with bacon.

4. Add stock or water to the frying pan and cook over a high heat, stirring all the brown crusty bits

from the sides of the pan into the stock. Skim if necessary and strain over the venison.

5. Add chopped onion, redcurrant jelly, *bouquet garni* and lemon juice, and season to taste with salt and freshly ground black pepper. Cover casserole and simmer venison gently for 2 to 2½ hours, until tender.

6. About 20 minutes before serving, add some small forcemeat balls made of sausagemeat mixed with egg and seasoned with dried herbs.

Hunter's Venison Stew

1.5 kg/3 lb venison
flour
3 Spanish onions, finely chopped
butter
225 g/8 oz unsmoked bacon, in 1 piece
6 cloves garlic
3 bay leaves
3 cloves
1 level teaspoon mixed dried herbs
   (marjoram, rosemary, thyme)
½ bottle red wine
3 large carrots, quartered
3 medium-sized potatoes, quartered

1. Trim sinews and bones from venison, and cut the meat into 5-cm/2-inch cubes. Roll them in flour.

2. Sauté onions in butter in a large flameproof casserole until soft. Remove from pan and reserve.

3. Dice unsmoked bacon, and sauté in remaining fat until golden. Remove and reserve.

4. Sauté venison in resulting fat until golden, then returned sautéed onions and bacon to casserole. Add garlic, bay leaves, cloves and dried herbs, and simmer, covered, in a cool oven (150°C, 300°F, Gas Mark 2) for 2 hours.

5. Reduce wine over a high heat to half the original quantity. Add to stew with quartered carrots and potatoes, and simmer for another hour.

84

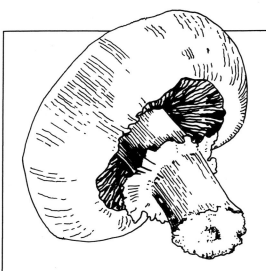

Jugged Hare

1 hare
18 small white onions
225 g/8 oz fat bacon, in 1 piece
2 level tablespoons butter or dripping
2 tablespoons olive oil
2 level tablespoons flour
1 bouquet garni (2 sprigs parsley, marjoram,
   1 bay leaf)
300 ml/½ pint red Burgundy
salt and freshly ground black pepper
2 level tablespoons tomato purée
100 g/4 oz mushrooms, quartered
vinegar

1. Ask your butcher to prepare hare, reserving the blood, which is a very necessary ingredient of this dish. Keep the saddle to serve roasted and cut remaining parts in serving pieces, chopping through the bones.

2. Peel onions and cut bacon into small thick strips. (If the bacon is very salty, the pieces should be blanched beforehand.)

3. Melt butter or dripping with oil in a thick-bottomed flameproof casserole and sauté onions and bacon until lightly browned. Remove onions and bacon, and reserve.

4. Put in the pieces of hare and brown them in the same fat. When coloured on all sides, sprinkle with flour and brown that also. Now add *bouquet garni* and wine, and enough water to cover. Season

to taste with salt, freshly ground black pepper and tomato purée. Simmer gently, covered, for 2½ to 3 hours, until hare is almost tender.

5. When ready, remove pieces of hare to a bowl and strain the sauce over them.

6. Return to a clean casserole; add onions, bacon and quartered mushrooms, and continue to simmer for 20 minutes, or until both the hare and vegetables are cooked through.

7. Then add the blood, mixed first with a little vinegar and some of the sauce. Strain it in beside the hare, mix well and bring to the boil. Be careful not to overboil it, or it will curdle.

Ragoût de Lapin

1 tender rabbit
18 button onions
12 shallots
3 level tablespoons butter
3 tablespoons olive oil
salt and freshly ground black pepper
2 level tablespoons flour
150 ml/¼ pint chicken stock
150 ml/¼ pint dry white wine
1 bouquet garni (2 sprigs parsley, 2 sprigs
   thyme, 1 stick celery, 2 bay leaves)
chopped fresh tarragon or parsley

1. Cut rabbit into serving pieces.

2. Sauté button onions and shallots in butter and olive oil until golden. Add rabbit pieces, season with salt and freshly ground black pepper, and sauté until well coloured. Transfer rabbit and vegetables to a flameproof casserole.

2. Add 2 level tablespoons flour to pan juices and stir until well blended. Add chicken stock and dry white wine and simmer, stirring continuously, until sauce has thickened. Add *bouquet garni*.
Note: If sauce is too thick, add a little more stock.

3. Pour sauce over rabbit pieces and vegetables, and simmer gently until rabbit is tender. Sprinkle with chopped fresh tarragon or parsley.

Guinea Fowl and Pheasants

Blanquette de Lapin

1 tender rabbit
½ lemon
1.15 litres/2 pints chicken or veal stock
1 Spanish onion, stuck with 2 cloves
4 carrots
1 bouquet garni (2 sprigs parsley, 2 sprigs
   thyme, 1 bay leaf)
rice
powdered saffron
2 level tablespoons butter
2 level tablespoons flour
2 egg yolks
150 ml/¼ pint double cream
juice of ½ lemon

1. Cut rabbit into serving pieces. Leave overnight in cold water with half a lemon.

2. Rinse well. Blanch meat by putting it in cold water and bringing it slowly to the boil. Skim carefully and drain.

3. Place blanched rabbit pieces in a deep flame-proof casserole with enough chicken or veal stock (or stock and water) to cover. Add a Spanish onion stuck with 2 cloves, 4 carrots cut into quarters lengthwise, and the *bouquet garni*, and bring to the boil. Skim, lower heat and simmer gently for 30 minutes. Add a handful of rice and a pinch of powdered saffron, and simmer until rabbit is tender.

4. Make a white *roux* by combining 2 level tablespoons butter and 2 level tablespoons flour in a saucepan. Add 600 ml/1 pint of stock from the rabbit and stir well over a high heat until the sauce is smooth and creamy. Lower heat and simmer for 15 minutes, stirring from time to time. Remove saucepan from heat and 'finish' sauce by stirring in egg yolks, cream and the juice of ½ lemon.

5. Drain the rabbit pieces from the remaining stock. Clean the casserole, return rabbit pieces to it and strain sauce over meat through a fine sieve. Keep warm in the oven with the casserole covered until ready to serve. A little more fresh cream and a squeeze of lemon may be added just before serving.

Lapin aux Pruneaux

1 tender rabbit
300 ml/½ pint red wine
4 carrots, sliced
1 Spanish onion, sliced
2 bay leaves
salt and freshly ground black pepper
2 level tablespoons butter
2 tablespoons olive oil
350 g/12 oz dried prunes, soaked in water
   overnight
2 level tablespoons redcurrant jelly

1. Cut rabbit into serving pieces.

2. Marinate pieces in red wine for 24 hours with sliced carrots and onion, bay leaves, and salt and freshly ground black pepper, to taste. Drain and pat dry with absorbent paper or a clean cloth.

3. Sauté pieces in butter and olive oil until they are well coloured.

4. Add marinade juices and enough water to cover. Add soaked prunes and bring to the boil. Skim carefully, lower heat and simmer gently for 1 hour, or until rabbit is tender.

5. Arrange rabbit pieces and prunes on a serving dish. Reduce the sauce over a high heat, correct seasoning, blend redcurrant jelly into sauce and pour over rabbit pieces.

Velouté Sauce (Chicken Velouté)

2 tablespoons butter
2 tablespoons flour
600 ml/1 pint chicken stock
salt
white peppercorns
mushroom peelings or stems
lemon juice

1. Melt butter in the top of a double saucepan, add flour and cook for a few minutes to form a pale *roux*. Add boiling stock, salt and peppercorns, and cook, stirring vigorously with a whisk until well blended.

2. Add mushroom peelings or stems, reduce heat and simmer gently, stirring occasionally and skimming from time to time, until the sauce is reduced to two-thirds of the original quantity and is thick but light and creamy. Flavour with lemon juice and strain through a fine sieve.

Note: This sauce forms the foundation of a number of the best white sauces, which take their distinctive names from the different ingredients added. Used by itself it is improved by the addition of a little double cream and egg yolk.

Basic Brown Sauce

2 tablespoons butter
1 small onion, thinly sliced
2 tablespoons flour
750 ml/1¼ pints well-flavoured brown stock
1 small carrot
1 small turnip
1 stick celery or ¼ teaspoon celery seed
4 mushrooms
2-4 tomatoes or 1-2 tablespoons tomato purée
1 bouquet garni (3 sprigs parsley, 1 sprig thyme, 1 bay leaf)
2 cloves
12 black peppercorns
salt

1. Heat butter in a thick-bottomed saucepan until it browns. Add thinly sliced onion and simmer, stirring constantly, until golden. Stir in flour and cook, stirring constantly, for a minute or two longer.

2. The good colour of your sauce depends upon the thorough browning of these ingredients without allowing them to burn. When this is accomplished, remove saucepan from the heat and pour in the stock; return to heat and stir until it comes to the boil. Allow to boil for 5 minutes, skimming all the scum from the top with a perforated spoon.

3. Wash and slice carrot, turnip, celery, mushrooms and tomatoes, and add them with the *bouquet garni*, cloves and peppercorns, and salt, to taste. Simmer the sauce gently for at least 30 minutes, stirring occasionally and skimming when necessary. Strain through a fine sieve and remove fat. Reheat before serving.

Basic Meat Aspic

225 g/8 oz beef bones
duck or chicken carcass, if available
1 calf's foot or 4 cleaned chicken feet
1 Spanish onion, sliced
1 large leek, sliced
2 large carrots, sliced
2 sticks celery, chopped
1.15 litres/2 pints water
salt and freshly ground black pepper
bouquet garni (sprig parsley, sprig thyme, bay leaf)
1 egg white
100 g/4 oz raw lean beef, chopped
1 teaspoon finely chopped chervil and tarragon

1. Combine first ten ingredients in a large stockpot, bring slowly to the boil and simmer gently for about 4 hours, removing scum from time to time. Strain and cool before skimming off the fat.

2. **To clarify the stock:** beat egg white lightly, and combine with chopped raw lean beef and chopped herbs in the bottom of a large saucepan. Add the cooled stock and mix well. Bring stock slowly to the boil, stirring constantly. Lower the

heat and simmer stock very gently for about 15 minutes. Strain through a flannel cloth while still hot. Allow stock to cool and then stir in one of the following:

Sherry Aspic
Stir in 4 tablespoons dry sherry.

Madeira Aspic
Stir in 4 tablespoons Madeira.

Port Aspic
Stir in 4 tablespoons port wine.

Tarragon Aspic
When clarifying aspic, add 6 additional sprigs of tarragon.

Note: Aspic will keep for several days in the refrigerator.

Béchamel Sauce

butter
½ onion, minced
2 tablespoons flour
600 ml/1 pint hot milk
2 tablespoons lean veal or ham, chopped
small sprig thyme
½ bay leaf
white peppercorns
freshly grated nutmeg

1. In a thick-bottomed saucepan, or in the top of a double saucepan, melt 2 tablespoons butter and cook onion in it over a low heat until transparent. Stir in flour and cook for a few minutes, stirring constantly, until mixture cooks through but does not take on colour.

2. Add hot milk and cook, stirring constantly, until the mixture is thick and smooth.

3. In another saucepan, simmer finely chopped lean veal or ham in 1 tablespoon butter over a

very low heat. Season with thyme, bay leaf, white peppercorns and grated nutmeg. Cook for 5 minutes, stirring to keep veal from browning.

4. Add veal to the sauce and cook over hot water for 45 minutes to 1 hour, stirring occasionally. When reduced to the proper consistency (two-thirds of the original quantity), strain sauce through a fine sieve into a bowl, pressing meat and onion well to extract all the liquid. Cover surface of sauce with tiny pieces of butter to keep film from forming.

For a richer Béchamel: remove saucepan from the heat, add 1 or 2 egg yolks, and heat through. Do not let sauce come to the boil after adding eggs or it will curdle.

Italian Tomato Sauce

2 Spanish onions, finely chopped
2 cloves garlic, finely chopped
4 tablespoons olive oil
6 tablespoons Italian tomato purée
1 (793-g/1 lb 12-oz) can Italian peeled
  tomatoes
2 bay leaves
4 tablespoons finely chopped parsley
¼ teaspoon oregano
1 small strip lemon peel
6 tablespoons dry white wine
salt and freshly ground black pepper
1-2 tablespoons Worcestershire sauce

1. Sauté finely chopped onions and garlic in olive oil in a large, thick-bottomed frying pan until transparent and soft but not coloured.

2. Stir in tomato purée and continue to cook for a minute or two, stirring constantly. Pour in Italian peeled tomatoes with their juice and add bay leaves, parsley, oregano and lemon peel. Add dry white wine, an equal quantity of water, and salt and freshly ground black pepper, to taste. Simmer gently, stirring from time to time, for 1 to 2 hours.

3. Just before serving, stir in Worcestershire sauce, to taste.

Index